Juvenile Responsibility & Law

THIRD EDITION

Law in Action Series

Juvenile Responsibility & Law

THIRD EDITION

Law in Action Series

Linda Riekes   Steve Jenkins   Armentha Russell

WEST PUBLISHING COMPANY
St. Paul   New York   Los Angeles   San Francisco

Composition: CompuText Productions
Copyediting: Jane Anderson
Cover: Leah Lewis-Westerfield
Illustrations: Leah Lewis-Westerfield, Robert D. Russell, Jr.,
and Robert E. Russell

Photographs: **11** James L. Shaffer; **30** Z. L. Ratliff, III; **31** Jane
Scherr/Jeroboam, Inc.; **57** Courtesy of the Library of
Congress; **79** Z. L. Ratliff, III; **99** Billy E. Barnes/
Jeroboam, Inc.; **131** Ed Reinke/AP Wide World Photos;
132 Z. L. Ratliff, III; **133** AP Wide World Photos; **170**
Z. L. Ratliff, III; **172** Z. L. Ratliff, III; **173** Billy E.
Barnes/Jeroboam, Inc.

Library of Congress Cataloging-in-Publication Data

Riekes, Linda.
    Juvenile responsibility and law / Linda Riekes, Armentha Russell, Steve
Jenkins, —3rd ed.
        p.   cm. —(Law in action series)
    Rev. ed. of: Juvenile problems and law. 2nd ed. ©1980.
    Summary: Presents common situations of juvenile delinquency and dis-
cusses the basic concepts of justice to be applied. Offers discussion and group
action on specific cases.
    ISBN 0-314-47363-7
    1. Juvenile courts—United States—Juvenile literature. 2. Juvenile justice,
Administration of—United States—Juvenile literature. [1. Juvenile delinquency.
2. Law. 3. Juvenile courts.] I. Russell, Armentha. II. Jenkins, Stephen. III.
Riekes, Linda. Juvenile problems and law. IV. Title. V. Series.
KF9780.R53 1990
345.73'08—dc 19   88-27656
[347.3058]   CIP
                                                                          AC

CONTENTS

CONTENTS

DEAR STUDENT:

Juvenile Responsibility and Law was written for you. The book is about the important place you have in our society today and the special responsibilities you have to yourself and to others. It is also about the role you play in shaping our country's future. Some of the first lessons in the book will help you to think about and carry out your responsibilities to yourself and to your family, friends, and community. Other lessons will help you to learn more about solving your own problems and being your own person.

The book will also help you to see and understand the special relationship that you as a young person have with our legal system. Some of the lessons tell the story of the juvenile court, how it began, and how it works today. You will learn about the history of the court, why it is set as it is, how it should work, and how it actually works in everyday life. Many people are concerned about today's juvenile court and are asking serious questions about how to deal with juveniles in the 1990s. We think it's important for you to understand the problems of trying to work out effective and fair ways of treating young people in the legal system. While the U.S. Constitution's Bill of Rights balances the rights of the individual and the rights of society, it is sometimes difficult to keep this balance. If you recognize and understand the difficulty, you will be able to work towards more just and responsible solutions.

And finally, many of the lessons will help you to see that your actions have consequences—that YOU can make a difference in your own life and in the lives of others around you at home, at school, and in your community. You are the future and the future is yours.

Sincerely,

Linda Riekes
Steve Jenkins
Armentha Russell

LESSON 1

Accepting Responsibility

Objectives

As a result of this lesson, students will be able to:

✧ Recognize that they are responsible for their own actions and the consequences of those actions.

✧ Analyze short- and long-range consequences of specific actions.

✧ Describe and analyze several different alternative actions for handling a particular situation and the possible consequences of those actions.

Every day, you are faced with **decisions** regarding what you might do in a variety of situations. You are responsible for making many of these decisions. You make decisions by choosing among a number of **alternative actions.**

Look at the statements at the top of the next page. Which of these young people are **responsible** for their own actions?

WHO'S RESPONSIBLE?

"I didn't do it. My brother made me do it."

"I can't handle math class. My teacher just doesn't explain math well to me."

"My goldfish died. My mom should have fed them."

"My future is wrecked. I didn't make the team. The coach doesn't like me."

"My friend said I had to do it. I had no choice."

The answer to the question of who is responsible is that each young person is responsible for his or her own actions, whether the person takes the **responsibility** or blames someone or something else.

For every action there is a **consequence**. Every time you decide to do something, there is a consequence or reaction to that action. For example, when someone rubs two sticks together, the person will probably get a reaction and create a fire. Look at the illustrations on the following pages, and identify each action and its possible consequences. Do you think the person in each illustration considered the consequences before deciding to act? Why? Why not? What are other possible consequences of each action?

Action

Possible Consequence(s)

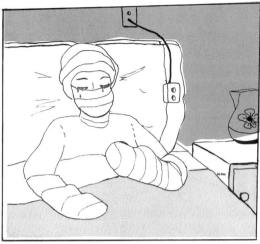

Action

Possible Consequence(s)

Think of an action that you have taken in the last week and **analyze** the consequences of it. How would the consequences have been different if you had not taken the action? What might have happened if you had chosen another alternative action?

Actions have both **short-** and **long-range consequences**. An example of a short- and long-range consequence would be if you didn't do your homework. The short-range consequence could be that you didn't get a grade on the paper. The long-range consequence is that the paper, with all the other missed assignments, would keep you from getting credit in the course; and you would not pass into the next grade. Look at the actions below. What might be the short and the long-range consequences for each action?

Susan decided that she would not go to class because she didn't have her science report finished, and it was due that day. The next day when asked by her teacher why she didn't have the report, Susan said that she had been sick.

George had been skipping school and hanging out with his older brother's friend.

Alberto was saving money from his job for a special summer course in an advanced computer science.

Kathy practices gymnastics everyday.

Look at each of the actions. What alternative actions could each of the people have made? How would those alternative decisions have changed the possible short and long-term consequences of each action?

Look at the drawings below and review each young person's alternatives. What might be other alternatives that each person could choose? What are the short- and long-range consequences for each alternative action? What additional information would you like to know about each situation, if you were making the decision?

A. Bob has to make a decision about where to live.

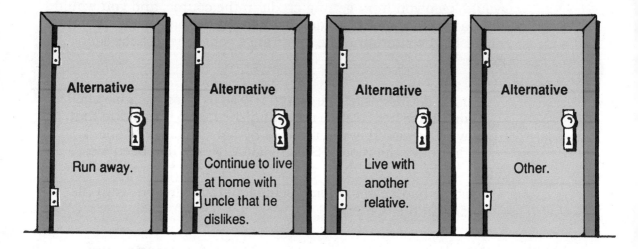

B. Jane has to make a decision about where to go to school.

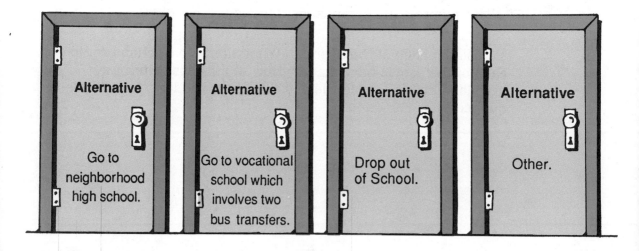

C. Alexandra has to decide whether to continue to go steady with her boyfriend of two years, or to meet and go out with others at school.

D. Josè has to decide if he should report a dealer who is selling drugs near his brother and sister's elementary school.

Carefully choosing between alternatives and thinking through the long- and short-range consequences is important for everyone to do. Some decisions don't work out. The person may have an opportunity to try another alternative. For example, in the drawing on the previous page, if the vocational high school Jane decided to choose does not work out, she might be able to transfer to another high school. Some decisions can be changed once they are made. Think of several decisions that are final decisions when, once made, there is really not an opportunity to change them.

A **juvenile court judge** said, "if young people would think about the consequences of their own actions and accept responsibility for those actions, I would see very few young people brought before me for illegal acts." Do you agree or disagree with the judge's statement? Explain your answer.

Make a bulletin board for your class, school, or community center which could be called "Consequences of Responsible Action." Draw pictures or write stories about responsible actions. Next to each story or picture develop another picture or story of a consequence of that responsible action.

·E X T R A·

Look for at least five articles in the newspaper and/or reports on television that deal with a person's actions. Make a four-column chart in your notebook to record the actions: 1) action, 2) short-range consequences, 3) long-range consequences, 4) my alternative action. The fourth column would list your alternative action if you have a better one than the one which was chosen.

✧ ✧ Vocabulary Words ✧ ✧

actions	juvenile court
alternative	long-range consequences
analyze	responsibility
consequence	responsible
decisions	short-range consequences
judge	

LESSON 2

Responsibility and Expectations

Objectives

As a result of this lesson, students will be able to:

✦ Identify and analyze the expectations their family, school, and community have for them.

✦ Explain the consequences of not meeting the expectations of family, school, and community.

✦ Identify expectations that peers have for one another and explain how those expectations may conflict with those that they hold for themselves and with their community.

✦ Recognize, apply, and practice refusal skills in dealing with peer expectations that are in conflict with their own and those of the community.

Every day, there are **expectations** of you. In school, with your family, and in the community, there are certain **rules** that you are expected to follow, certain **goals** that you are supposed to achieve, and certain behavior that others expect of you.

Some expectations come from the community. For example, you are expected not to talk loudly in a movie theater. You are expected not to "crash" or "jump" ahead of the person in front of you in a store or theater line. People are expected to obey family and school rules. They are also expected to obey the **laws** of their community. For example, you are not expected to litter or destroy another person's property. Think of some other rules and laws you are expected to follow each day.

It is your responsibility to understand the consequences of your not choosing to live up to different expectations for your behavior. Read the situations below involving one fifteen-year-old student, John, *at school, with his family*, and *in the community*. Then answer the questions that follow.

A. John's mother asks him to stay with his younger brother while she goes to the store. While he is staying with his younger brother, he gets a call from his best friend who wants him to go to a party in twenty minutes.

B. John's father doesn't like all of John's friends. He wants John to go out only with those who meet with his approval. One of the friends that John's father doesn't like asked John to go to a big party which John really wants to attend.

C. John's school requires a "C" average to be on a school athletic team. John loves baseball, but he has trouble with several subjects in school.

D. In John's school there is a rule that a student cannot be tardy more than twice, or have more than two unexcused absences a semester. Students who break this rule must meet with the assistant principal. John has been tardy twice this semester.

E. The neighborhood store next to John's school has posted the following sign on its door: "Shoplifters will be **prosecuted**."

F. The **curfew** in the city where John lives is 9:00 p.m. for anyone under 17 during school nights or weeknights (Sunday through Thursday) and 11:00 p.m. on weekends (Friday and Saturday).

What expectations do John's parents have for John? What are the school's expectations? What are some of the community's expectations? Why do John's parents have these expectations? Why does the school have these expectations? Why does the community have these expectations? If you were John's parents or the principal of the school, what should be the consequence or consequences in each situation if expectations are not met?

How can you handle expectations that you think are unfair or unreasonable? Explain your answer. If you can't get someone to change his or her mind and the expectation still exists, how do you handle the situation? Why? What if you disagree with an expectation of the school or community? How, then, do you handle the situation?

Read the statement below about John and his friends and answer the questions that follow.

"I would like to be a baseball player. I really am a great pitcher. I can really throw. I am also a good batter. Not many famous pitchers are good batters, but I really am good. My friends say that I'm crazy because only one in a million gets to be a major league or even a minor league pitcher. They say the best thing I can do for myself is just to enjoy life now. My friends want me to hang out with them. Some of my friends are into drugs and getting drunk. I'm not into that stuff, but they expect me to be."

1. What are John's expectations for himself?

2. What must he do to achieve his goal?

3. What are the short-term things that he must do?

4. What are the long-term things that he must do?

5. Explain how you feel about what John's friends said to him about being a pitcher.

6. How do John's friends' expectations for him conflict with what the community expects him to do? Explain your answer.

7. How do John's friends' expectations of John conflict with his own expectations?

Read the story below about Maria and answer the questions that follow.

> Maria had moved to a new city with her mother and brothers. She loves art and wants to be an artist. At her new school there is an honors art program. Maria wants to be in that program next year. Maria has a new best friend, Jennifer, at the school. Jennifer is really popular, and Maria was very glad that Jennifer liked her. One afternoon when they were at the mall, Maria saw Jennifer take some earrings from a counter and put them in her purse without paying for them. Later at lunch, Jennifer showed the earrings to Maria and said, "Here, these are for you. You can get me some next time. It's easy. I'll show you."

1. What are Maria's expectations for herself?

2. What is Maria's main goal, and what must she do to achieve her goal?

3. What are the short-term things that she must do?

4. What are the long-term things that she must do?

5. Explain how you feel about what Maria's friend Jennifer wants her to do.

6. How do her friend's expectations conflict with what the community expects her to do? Explain your answer.

7. How do Jennifer's expectations of Maria conflict with Maria's expectations of herself?

If you decide that you disagree with your **peers'** expectations of you, how would you refuse to do what they want? The following are some **refusal skills** that you can use to help you handle peer **pressure.** Many times you can use more than one refusal skill at a time. Review the picture stories on the next page. Choose one or more of the refusal skills below, or develop one or more of your own, that could be used to handle each situation.

After selecting the refusal skills, answer the following: Why did you choose the skills that you chose? What are the short-range consequences if the person did not refuse? What are the long-range consequences?

REFUSAL SKILLS

Give excuse or reason.	"My parents won't let me out of the house," or "My family is going to visit . . ." or "I'm busy."
Change the subject.	Start talking about something else.
Reverse the pressure.	When someone is trying to talk you into doing something that you don't want to do, try to talk him or her out of it.

Ignore.   Don't pay any attention.

Avoid.   Don't go where you know there is a person who might have expectations of you that are in conflict with yours. Stay away from possible trouble.

Offer another plan.   "Why don't we go ____ instead?"
"Why don't we do ____ instead?"

Just leave.   "I'm leaving."

If you were the person in each picture below, what refusal skill might you use in each situation? What would you say or do?

Activity #1

Does your school have a booklet that describes its expectations (the rules, responsibilities and rights) of its students? If not, you can work with your principal to develop such a booklet of the expectations that the school has for its students. If your school does have such a book, you can do a chart which describes the expectations, the reason for each expectation, and the consequences if the expectation is not met.

Activity #2

Younger students often look up to older students. You can be a good example for younger students by helping them learn how to refuse a peer or an older student who has expectations that are in conflict with their own or those of their community. With the help of your teacher, you may arrange to give class presentations for elementary students. You may help them make a poster or do a booklet emphasizing the refusal skills you taught them.

E X T R A

There are many different local and national organizations that are trying to help young people learn to refuse expectations of adults and peers that conflict with those of the community. Contact these organizations and read about the programs that they have and the information they offer.

✧ ✧ Vocabulary Words ✧ ✧

curfew
expectations
goals
laws
peers

pressure
prosecuted
refusal skills
rules

LESSON 3

Problem-Solving Strategies

Objectives

As a result of this lesson, students will be able to:

✧ Identify steps in one problem-solving strategy.

✧ Analyze the need for different steps in a problem-solving strategy.

✧ Practice using a problem-solving strategy in specific situations.

Refusal skills can help you in dealing with the expectations of others. The skills can help you to take responsibility for what you want to do, and to learn how to **solve** your problems. Everyone has problems at one time or another. Sometimes people don't try to solve their problems because they don't want to, don't know how to, or perhaps are waiting for someone else to solve them. There are many kinds of problems. There are personal problems, community problems, scientific or mathematical problems, and problems of inventors, just to name a few.

To be a good problem-solver, you have to develop a problem-solving **strategy** that works for you. A strategy is a step-by-step **process** that helps you find the best possible solution to the problem. Keep in mind that some problems are extremely complicated and can't be handled alone. Also, you can try to help someone else to solve his or her problem, and you can try to get help with your problems, but everybody has to make his or her *final* decision on what action to take about a problem.

Look at the cartoon below. What do you think of the problem-solving strategy? Do you think it is realistic? Why? Why not?

PROBLEM ??? SOLUTION

The illustration on page 18 shows one problem-solving strategy. It breaks down a problem-solving strategy into steps. Different people may organize these steps somewhat differently, or they may have slightly different names for each step. But a step-by-step process, whatever the name of the steps you use, can be very helpful. In this lesson the steps look like the picture on page 18.

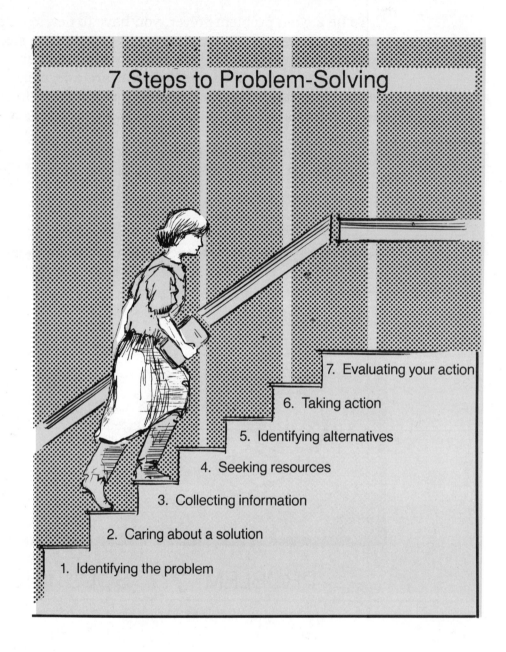

7 Steps to Problem-Solving

7. Evaluating your action

6. Taking action

5. Identifying alternatives

4. Seeking resources

3. Collecting information

2. Caring about a solution

1. Identifying the problem

Step 1. Identifying the Problem.

This sounds like an easy step, but it really is a crucial step. Everyone sees problems in different ways. Different people can look at the same information and not be able to agree on what they see. For example, look at the figures below. What do you think is the correct answer for each figure? If you look carefully, you will find that everything is not as it seems at first glance.

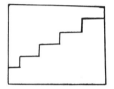   Is this right side up or upside down?

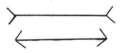   Which line is longer?

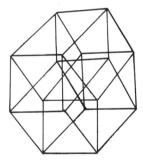   How many cubes are there?

People may share the same problem but see it from totally different **perspectives**. The problem may not be what it appears when you first look at it. For example, you get very angry with your brother because he took something out of your room without your permission. The real problem is you might be angry because your brother made better grades or made a team you wanted to make or got more attention. **Identifying** the problem requires you to analyze it. *Why is it important to be able to identify the problem clearly?*

Step 2. Caring about a Solution.

Before you go any further in the problem-solving strategy, you must decide if you really care about solving the problem that has been identified. Read the story below.

> During the eighth-grade lunch period, several students were fighting and name-calling. Other students gathered around to watch and urge on the "fighters." After the fight was stopped, the counselor had a meeting with all the eighth-grade students to discuss the problem. In the course of the discussion, some of the students said the fighting and name-calling gave everyone "something to do after they ate lunch." They said they really didn't care about solving the problem because they liked watching the fights. Other students said that part of the reason there was so much fighting and name-calling, was that other students watched and gave the "fighters" an audience. The counselor reminded the students of the school's expectations of good behavior. She told the students to think about the serious consequences they would face if they caused disruptions during lunch. The counselor and the students discussed the consequences and then **brainstormed** possible solutions to the problem. As a group, the students voted to ignore any fighting and name-calling. One student said, "Let's agree to not pay any attention to the fights. If the 'fighters' get caught, it'll be their problem, and they will have to face the consequences." Two weeks after the students had met and voted, fighting was almost non-existent during the eighth-grade lunch period.
>
> If the class had decided that they didn't care about the problem, could the problem have been solved? Explain your answer. *Why is caring about a solution an important step in problem-solving?*

Step 3. Collecting More Information.

You think you have identified the problem, you care about solving it, and now you need information on how to solve it. At this step you need to ask yourself these questions:

✧ What more do I need to know about the problem?

✧ Where can I get more information?

✧ Who might be helpful in getting me more information?

✧ Who can help me with this problem?

Why is collecting more information an important step?

Step 4. Seeking Resources.

This step involves using the information that you've obtained in Step 3 to help you seek **resources** to solve the problem. What are the different resources you can use? Look at some possible resources below.

✧ School counselor

✧ Youth hotline number for emergency calls

✧ Parent

✧ Relative

✧ Teacher

✧ Religious leader

✧ Peer

✧ Older brother, sister, cousin

✧ Community center

✧ Librarians who are able to provide books that describe situations where other young people have dealt with that problem

✧ Law enforcement official(s)

What additional resources can you think of that are not on the list? Why is seeking resources an important step?

Step 5. Identifying Alternatives.

Begin by brainstorming as many alternative actions as you can think of in trying to solve a problem. List all the ways—do not leave out any. After you have identified the different ways that you could act, it is important to consider both the long and short-range consequences of each action. After collecting the information, working with different resources, and carefully analyzing what you think the short and long-term consequences could be, you will be able to make a responsible choice among your alternatives.

Why is identifying alternatives an important step?

Step 6. Taking Action.

The next step in the problem-solving strategy is to take action. Sometimes people decide that they are not going to do anything about a problem, as in the following statements:

1. I think my finger is infected, but I don't have time to deal with it. It will just heal on its own.

2. My little brother is too close to the stove. I'm sure he won't get burned.

3. I really want to be in the special program, but I'll just take my chances that I'll be selected.

Deciding not to take action, as in the three examples above, is really taking action. When you don't take responsibility for your action, whatever happens, the action will still affect you, and there will still be consequences for you and possibly others.

Why is taking action an important step?

7. Evaluating Your Action.

It is very important to review your action and to see whether it turned out to be a good solution to your problem. Hopefully it was, but if not, what can you learn from the experience for your next problem? How would you handle the problem differently next time? What did you learn?

*Why is **evaluating** your action an important step?*

Using the problem-solving strategy you have just learned, practice problem-solving with the following five problems. Take each problem through the first five steps.

You will not be able to take action or evaluate your action, but you will be able to see how you could use the other steps in this problem-solving strategy.

Problem #1

"I'm never going back to school. Just because I'm the biggest in my class, the teacher is always picking on me. She asks me to carry books, move furniture, or carry movie equipment. I know I'm not a great student, but she takes advantage of me. I'm never carrying anything else, ever! I'm not going back to that class."

Problem #2

"I used to get drunk with my friends. I got messed up pretty bad a few times and decided not to drink any more. I still like my friends, but they don't like me because they say I'm a goody-goody. I don't know what to do."

Problem #3

"Two of my friends just can't get along. They want me to choose between them. I like both of them."

Problem #4

"One of my best friends is **shoplifting** at the mall. My mother is a police officer and has been talking about the crackdown on shoplifting at the mall. My friend is going to the mall today."

Problem #5

"My best friend's mother died in a car crash. I want to help my friend, but I don't know what to do."

MAKING A DIFFERENCE

Every community has different kinds of resources available to young people to help with problem-solving. What resources are available in your community? Sometimes there are help centers in a community that many people do not know about. You can help yourself, your class and other young people by conducting a survey of your community to discover what kinds of resources are available for young people and then helping the organization publicize its services. In order to publicize the services of the centers you will need to ask the center or centers the following questions:

1. What kind of services does your help center include?

2. Does your center serve only a certain age group? If so, what ages are serviced?

3. Where is the center located, and what hours is it open?

4. Who staffs the center?

5. Must people make an appointment?

6. Is there any fee involved? If so, what is the fee?

7. What are the center's rules?

8. Do you have a pamphlet about the center? If not, would a pamphlet be helpful?

Talk with the center's director about how you could publicize information about the center's services (for example, by designing a pamphlet or making posters to hang in public places).

------------------------------- · E X T R A · -------------------------------

Activity #1

Ask a math teacher and a science teacher at your school to explain problem-solving strategies in their subjects. How are their different problem-solving strategies similar to the ones described in this chapter? How are they different? You might want to read about how an inventor or a scientist goes about solving his or her problem.

Activity #2

Throughout this text, you will have an opportunity to express your opinions on juvenile responsibility and the law. Begin a journal, "My Thoughts on Juvenile Responsibility and Law" and write your thoughts about juveniles based on what you are reading and studying. You may wish to make comments on the opinions expressed by other students, or comments based on news stories or actual discussions with juvenile judges, attorneys, law enforcement officers, friends, and family members. Review your journal from time to time to see if your opinions have changed. If they have changed, explain your reasons.

✧ ✧ **Vocabulary Words** ✧ ✧

brainstormed   **resources**
evaluating   **shoplifting**
identifying   **solve**
perspectives   **strategy**
process

LESSON 4

Responsibility and Your Peers

Objectives

As a result of this lesson, students will be able to:

✦ Explain some responsible ways of helping their peers with problems.

✦ Explain the need for counseling skills used in problem-solving.

✦ Analyze two problem situations and apply a problem-solving strategy and counseling skills.

You can't usually solve the problems of another person, but you may be able to help that person with some of the steps in a problem-solving strategy. There are some problems that another person may have where you can't do much to help, except to be a good and supportive friend. The following is a true story about some young people who took responsibility for helping their peers with problem-solving. Their story appears below.

Aisha Newman, Peter Baker, and George Tanizaki were good friends who were always getting into trouble at school and in the community. They were known as "troublemakers" at school and were frequent visitors to the principal's office. Other students called Aisha, Peter, and George the "experts" in knowing how to handle many problems. Peers in their school who had problems started to come to them for advice. The three heard some problems that were really serious. They knew that some of the problems were too big for them to handle alone. They had an idea that there should be a place where young people could go for help with problems. The place could offer peer counseling. The counseling would be done by young people with advice and resources from adult counselors. They talked to Mr. Johnson, their favorite teacher, about the idea. Mr. Johnson explained to them that he felt they should start by not getting into any more trouble themselves. He said, "Your friends and others in school look at you as really special, and you should be models for them."

He also talked to them about their ideas. After a lot of talking, planning, and hard work, they got their peer help center started. They named it the HELP Center. Soon young people with many different kinds of problems called or came into the Center.

Working with the advice of adults, a board of directors of young people set up a variety of different rules for the Center. For example, one of the rules was that the peer counselors had to stay out of trouble themselves. Five of the rules are described in the following excerpt from the HELP Center handbook.

RULE 1

You must never put anyone down about his or her problems. You should learn different ways of building someone's **self-esteem** rather than to tear someone down. Every counselor must work with a trained adult counselor to help build self-esteem in the people whom you are trying to help. Poor self-esteem can be a problem by itself. It can make someone feel down and distrustful, worry that something is wrong with him or her, and be uncomfortable with people. Poor self-esteem leads people to do anything to be accepted, to be part of the "Group."

RULE 2

You must have training in listening and questioning skills to be a HELP counselor. Adult counselors can be very important in your learning and practicing these skills. Being an active listener takes practice. Learning to ask **appropriate** questions is also extremely important.

RULE 3

You need to know other resource youth centers in the community, including drug and substance abuse centers, tutoring centers, and places where students can get other services they might need.

RULE 4

Everything that you hear in the Center you must keep in strict **confidence.** Trust is a crucial element in counseling and everyone who comes to the Center must know that whatever is said in the Center never leaves.

RULE 5

HELP counselors must work toward developing **empathy**. They should try to put themselves in someone else's shoes. Sometimes that is quite difficult. Perhaps that person is really inconsiderate of others and acts selfishly. The person could be really hard to relate to, but part of being an effective counselor is trying to understand the other person's problem and his or her point of view.

The rules on page 28 are just some of the **requirements** that each counselor at the HELP Center must follow. Review the rules. Why do you think each rule was made? What are some of the skills that counselors had to learn? Why do you think those skills are important? Since these are just a few of the rules, what other rules would you have? Why?

The next pages describe two cases brought to HELP. The pictures in the book and the names are not the real ones, but the cases are real. The story about Tony might actually have been about a girl and the story of Leslie might actually have been about a boy. Study the two cases and answer the questions that follow each one. Use the problem-solving strategy from Lesson 3 for each case. In Tony's situation, keep in mind that a parent has certain responsibilities and that a young person has certain responsibilities to his or her parents. What are those responsibilities? In looking at Leslie's situation, think about the responsibilities that a teacher has to a student and a student has to a teacher. What are those responsibilities?

PROBLEM 1

Tony

"I am 14 years old. I want to leave home because my mother is impossible to live with. She thinks she can dish out all the orders—telling me when to be home and always asking me about who my friends are. My mother is always yelling at me, and I yell back. I don't need her telling me what to do. I want to leave and start living my own life."

Tony's mother

"Tony gets angry quickly. I want what's best for him. I hear of so many problems with drinking, drugs, and trouble with police that children his age get involved with, it causes me to worry. I realize he wants more freedom. I do care whether or not he gets into trouble. It's been hard for me to handle him ever since his father left. I don't know exactly when it's best to leave him on his own and when to force him to obey my rules; but I cannot stand it when he talks back and does not show respect. If only we could talk without him losing his temper."

✧ What are Tony's feelings?

✧ What is the problem as Tony sees it?

✧ What are his mother's feelings?

✧ What is the problem as his mother sees it?

✧ What suggestions can you make that might help Tony and his mother handle their problem?

PROBLEM 2

Ms. Mendez

"At first Leslie seemed bored in class. I could tell she didn't like history. When we talked about it, she said she didn't think she was good in history, so she didn't try. After a while in my class, she seemed to like history better. Her tests improved greatly. I was very pleased with her progress and told her so. I decided to give her a "B" for the course. I wanted to be fair to all the students in the class. I have a standard of what I consider "A" work. Some of the students met my standards and got an "A". Leslie did not meet these standards. I didn't think it was fair to give her an "A", even though I was happy with her progress."

Leslie

"When I started Ms. Mendez' history course, I hated history. I had only gotten "D's" from most of my other teachers. Ms. Mendez was nice and talked to me a lot about interesting things in history. I started doing the assignments and Ms. Mendez kept telling me how pleased she was with my improvement. I was really happy and thought for sure I would get an "A" for the course. I'm angry now because she only gave me a "B", and I think I deserved an "A"! I did all that work! She makes me so mad, I don't feel like talking to her again."

✧ What was Ms. Mendez' position about giving Leslie an "A"?

✧ Do you think it was a hard decision for her to make? Explain your answer.

✧ What was Leslie's point of view?

✧ How did she feel when she received a "B"?

✧ What are some ways that Leslie and Ms. Mendez might deal with this problem?

MAKING A DIFFERENCE

Your counselor could help your class with developing listening and questioning skills or improving your problem-solving strategy. Working with your counselor, you could contact your school's parent organization. Ask them if you could assist in presenting a program for parents and students on listening and questioning skills, or do a problem-solving strategy by role playing Tony's and Leslie's cases.

· E X T R A ·

Ask your librarian for suggestions about non-fiction and fiction books which deal with a problem that interests you, and read one of those books. Or you might want to read both a fiction and a non-fiction book on the problem you have chosen and compare how the two authors handle the subject.

✧ ✧ Vocabulary Words ✧ ✧

appropriate
confidence
empathy

requirements
self-esteem

LESSON 5

Responsible Citizenship And The Law

Objectives

As a result of this lesson, students will be able to:

✧ Explain that laws affect them every day in a number of important ways.

✧ Explain how the United States Constitution affects their lives.

✧ Identify some ways they can exercise their responsibility as citizens by influencing the lawmaking process.

The following is an excerpt from a "diary" written by an eighth grade student. It is called "A Day Without Laws."

My Diary - February 25

I woke up and came down to breakfast. I opened my cereal and bugs poured out. My mother said that she had just bought the cereal, but since there were no more laws, there was nothing that she could do about it. I asked her what time it was. She said that the lawmakers in Washington used to set the time and since they stopped making laws and went home, she didn't know the time. The people who enforce the laws went home, too, she said. I went upstairs and decided not to think about it. I went back to bed because there was no school. I didn't know what to do.

Try to imagine what a day without any laws would be like for you. If you were to write your own "My Day Without Laws" what would you say?

Look at the following events in the day of a young person. Then answer the questions that follow.

JANUARY

Monday

Getting out of bed
Taking a shower
Eating breakfast
Listening to the radio
Reading the newspaper
Watching television
Talking to a parent or guardian
Walking or riding to school
Participating in a fire drill at school
Eating lunch
Playing in the park

1. Which of these events have something to do with laws? Why?

2. Which events are not affected by laws? Why?

3. If you were describing your day, what other events might you add? Which of these additional events have something to do with the law? Why? Which ones do not? Why?

The law affects you every day in very important ways. For example, the law in your state tells you how many days you must attend school each year. It also tells you how old you must be before you can drive a car.

What other ways can you think of that the law affects your everyday life?

Imagine that you are reading a newspaper and you find the following headline:

U.S. CONGRESS PROPOSES BILL THAT SCHOOL WILL BE OPEN 365 DAYS A YEAR

You go to read the article and find that not only is **Congress** proposing a **bill** that says school will be open 365 days a year, but anyone ages 6 to 18 not attending will be **fined** $500 or spend six months in jail. Furthermore, any person caught complaining or criticizing the new law may be arrested, immediately convicted without a trial, and sentenced to pay a fine or sent to jail for speaking out against the law.

What do you think about this bill? Would it be fair? Why?

What would YOU do about this bill if you thought it was unjust? Compare your answers to those given by three other students.

"I would go to my teacher and ask her what to do. This is a **democracy** and no one can do that to me."

"The **United States Constitution** provides for electing **lawmakers** and government leaders. So I would talk with the President or Congressperson and see what could be done."

"I would go to jail because there is nothing that can be done about this law."

Would this law **violate** the U.S. Constitution? If so, how?

THE IMPORTANCE OF THE U.S. CONSTITUTION

The United States Constitution is the basic law of our nation. The Constitution, and the **amendments** to it, say:

✧ That people have basic rights and the government should protect those rights.

✧ How the government is to be set up.

✧ How laws are to be made and changed.

✧ How the individuals who serve in government are to be chosen.

On September 17, 1987, the Constitution was 200 years old. It is the oldest written document of its kind in the world. Under the Constitution, the source of power became "We, the People." No laws made in the United States may conflict with the Constitution. Under our Constitution, the courts have exercised the power to determine whether a law is **unconstitutional**. The Constitution has withstood the test of time. Yet, each generation must protect the rights and privileges given to us; otherwise, through carelessness or indifference, these freedoms may vanish.

The first ten amendments to the U.S. Constitution are called the **Bill of Rights**. These amendments protect our most basic rights such as freedom of speech and freedom of religion.

Turn to the Bill of Rights in the back of your book. How many of these amendments would be violated by the proposed school law on page 35? Use the following chart to help you analyze whether or not the law violates each amendment.

		Yes	No
AMENDMENT	1:	?	?
AMENDMENT	2:	?	?
AMENDMENT	3:	?	?
AMENDMENT	4:	?	?
AMENDMENT	5:	?	?
AMENDMENT	6:	?	?
AMENDMENT	7:	?	?
AMENDMENT	8:	?	?
AMENDMENT	9:	?	?
AMENDMENT	10:	?	?

What can YOU do about unjust laws? Do you agree or disagree with the following actions suggested by other students? Explain your answer.

"I wouldn't do anything. The law is not my problem."

"Only adults can do something about the law."

"I would find out who makes the laws and try to change their minds."

There are lots of ways to **influence** lawmakers and the lawmaking process. This is called **lobbying**.

Anyone who voices an opinion to a lawmaker is, in a sense, a **lobbyist**. Lobbying for a special interest in government is one way YOU can take part in the lawmaking process. Any laws or proposed laws that affect you should be of special interest to you.

What are some laws that affect you as a young person? What about laws dealing with the environment? With animals? What else?

Look at the picture below. What are the special interests of each of these people?

There are citizen lobbyists and professional lobbyists. Professional lobbyists are hired by groups of people with similar interests. Many citizen and professional lobbyists influence lawmaking by *talking directly to someone in the government.* However, there are many other ways to influence lawmakers, such as *writing letters to lawmakers* and *writing letters to your local paper supporting your special interest.* Other ways to lobby are *getting a* **petition** *drive going* and *working on getting lists of people who are "for" or "against" a bill or law.* Other ways include *holding an open meeting and inviting a lawmaker to listen to the concerns of citizens on a bill or law.*

Briefly describe how each of the above italicized lobbying strategies influence lawmakers. What other ways of influencing lawmakers can you think of?

A responsible citizen works for the kind of laws he or she wants and works against those that he or she does not. Write a sample letter to your U.S. Representative or U.S. Senator providing the reasons that he or she should not support the 365 day school bill. Communicate your reasons in a way that you think will effectively influence him or her.

Look at the picture below. What might the picture tell you about lobbying?

What are ways that responsible citizens can work together to influence lawmakers? Develop a plan of action, besides individual letter writing, to influence lawmakers on any bill or law you think is important.

Look at the list of bills below. Select one (or develop a proposed bill of your own) and design a plan of action to influence lawmakers to support it.

A bill to:

✧ Develop a new recreational center in your area

✧ Provide additional assistance to the homeless

✧ Provide more day care facilities for working parents

✧ Develop placement programs for stray animals

MAKING A DIFFERENCE

Write to some of the lawmakers in your state and ask them what kind of lobbying activities they think are most effective. You may wish to explain to lawmakers that you are studying responsible citizenship and lawmaking. Their responses may give you some additional ideas of ways you can participate in the lawmaking process. Using the information you receive from the lawmakers, develop a one-page summary of the information they provide. Share your summary with other students and organizations in your community.

· E X T R A ·

Call or write the League of Women Voters and other groups dealing with lawmakers in your community to request information on effective lobbying techniques. Compare the suggestions you receive with the plan of action you developed earlier.

✧ ✧ Vocabulary Words ✧ ✧

amendments
Bill of Rights
bill
Congress
democracy
fine
influence

lawmakers
lobbying
lobbyist
petition
unconstitutional
United States Constitution
violate

LESSON 6

Responsible Citizenship and the Government

Objectives

As a result of this lesson, students will be able to:

✧ Recognize and discuss the importance of being a citizen lobbyist.

✧ Recognize and discuss the importance of knowing information about the three branches of government at the local, state, and federal levels.

✧ Explain the functions of different branches and levels of government.

If you saw the following headlines, where would you go to lobby?

1.   *U.S. Congress Proposes Bill That School Will Be Open 365 Days a Year*

2.   *STATE EDUCATION REQUIREMENTS CHANGE—STUDENTS NEED 10 MORE YEARS TO GRADUATE*

3.   City Ordinance Changes—Parks Closing at 3:30 P.M.

4.   NEW SPEED ZONES IN EFFECT NEAR CITY SCHOOLS

5.   *New Draft Law in Effect for 12 Year Olds*

6.   **PROPOSED STATUTE RAISES LEGAL DRIVING AGE TO 35**

As a citizen lobbyist, you need to know a number of different things in order to influence the appropriate lawmakers in each of these examples. One of the first things you need to know is that there are three different **levels of government—Federal, State,** and **Local.**

The following section will help you identify which levels of government would likely prepare the above laws.

LEVELS OF GOVERNMENT

The writers of the Constitution wanted to have a government in which there was one central authority that could keep the states working together but would also allow the states and local governments to have powers of their own. Today, most people must deal with three levels of government.

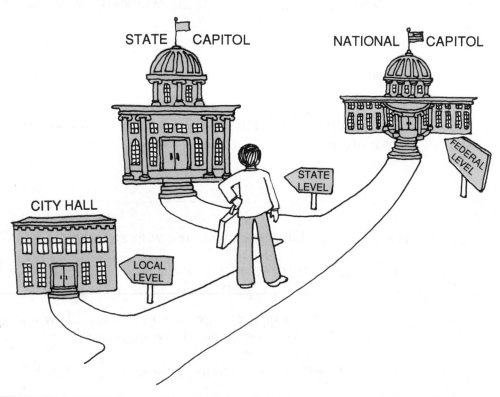

Federal (National)

The President, Congress, and most of the federal (national) agencies are located in Washington, DC. However, many of the federal agencies have regional offices throughout the country. The federal government is responsible for what affects the nation as a whole, such as:

✧ National defense

✧ Postal system

✧ Money and business between states and with other countries

✧ Regulating transportation between the states

✧ Maintaining the U.S. highway system

State

The state governments are located in the capitol city of each state. They handle concerns affecting people living in the state, such as:

✧ State roads

✧ Marriage and divorce laws

✧ State parks

✧ Requirements for licensing doctors, lawyers, and other professionals

✧ Education

Local

The local governments are located in cities, towns, and counties. They handle problems directly affecting the people living in a particular city, town, or county, such as:

✧ Providing police and fire protection

✧ Housing and zoning laws

✧ Local traffic laws

✧ Some parks and recreational sites

✧ Garbage and trash pick up

Can you match each headline on pages 41 and 42 with the right level of government?

	Federal	State	Local
1.	?	?	?
2.	?	?	?
3.	?	?	?
4.	?	?	?
5.	?	?	?
6.	?	?	?

As an active citizen lobbyist, you are concerned with making sure that laws you think are not in your best interest or the interests of society are not passed in the first place. You are also concerned with **repealing** laws that have been already passed but are against your best interest or the interests of society. You must also be concerned with laws that DO serve your best interests and those of society. You must be concerned with how those laws are carried out and how they are **enforced**. In order to be an effective lobbyist for all aspects of the legal process, it is important to understand the different **branches of government** and their responsibilities under the law. The next section will help you understand the roles and responsibilities of the three major branches of government.

BRANCHES OF GOVERNMENT

The founding fathers (women did not have the opportunity to be lawmakers at that time), who wrote the United States Constitution, feared a government that could be ruled by one person or one powerful group. To make certain that all power did not go to one person, they put together a plan that separated the government into three branches: **Legislative, Executive,** and **Judicial**.

The Constitution gives each of these branches special powers which the other branches do not have. In this way one branch is supposed to check the other branches by balancing any overload of power. This is called the system of "checks and balances." The "power" comes from the people.

Look at the drawing on the next page . Explain how you are part of the "power" as a citizen of the United States.

The system of the three branches has generally produced a stable, strong, and responsive government. However, there are problems which arise even though these branches try to work together. There are branches at each level—local, state, and federal.

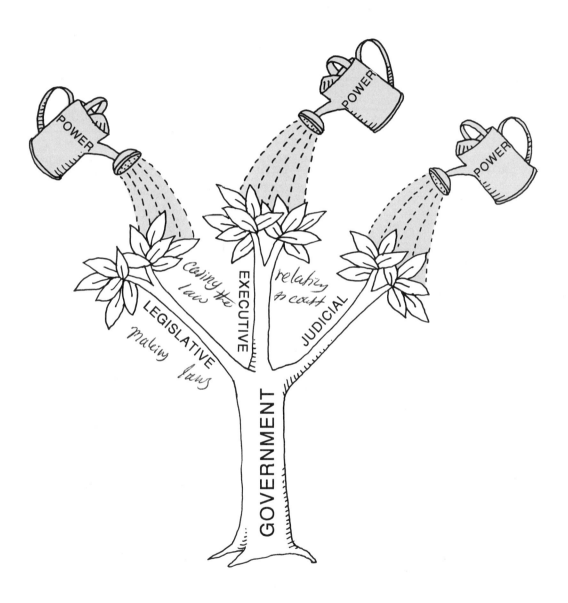

Look at the chart dealing with the federal level on the next page and describe how the branches balance each other.

BRANCHES (at the Federal level)	WHO WORKS THERE	WHAT THEY DO (Responsibilities)
Executive	President. Vice President. Cabinet members. People who work in departments and agencies.	Carry out laws. The Federal agencies and departments make federal regulations and see that laws are enforced. President can veto (reject) a law and also can propose a law.
Legislative	Senators—Senate. Representatives—in the House of Representatives. Senate and House make up Congress.	Make, change, and repeal laws. Congress can override a presidential veto by 2/3 vote of its members.
Judicial	Supreme Court Justices. Federal judges. Appeals Court judges.	**Interpret** and define what laws mean in specific cases. Determine if any laws are unconstitutional.

The following is a list of important information about government. Explain why a young person might want to know this information.

1. The names of your local lawmakers.

2. Where to write your local lawmakers.

3. How to register to vote.

4. Who appoints the head of your local law enforcement organization.

5. The dates of the next elections for the **United States Senate** and **House of Representatives** in your state.

6. The dates of the next elections for your local council person and your mayor.

7. How school board members are chosen.

8. The date of the next election for the governor of your state.

What other information can you think of that young people should know about their government?

Activity #1

For a specific period of time, read the newspaper or listen to the news on radio or television that involves the branches of government. Keep a record of the news items you hear or read about. Bring your news items to class. With your items and those of your classmates, make a class chart like the one at the top of the next page. Put each news item in the correct space on the chart.

	LOCAL LEVEL	STATE LEVEL	FEDERAL LEVEL
EXECUTIVE BRANCH			
LEGISLATIVE BRANCH			
JUDICIAL BRANCH			

Activity #2

Research the important information about government on the previous page. Add additional information you think is important for responsible citizens to know. Organize the information into a fact sheet and share it with other students and neighborhood groups.

·E X T R A·

Knowing the people who serve in the three branches of government in your city, state, and in Washington, D.C. will make you a more informed citizen. It will also give you the information you need to take an active part in influencing the lawmaking process.

To help you learn more about the people who serve in government, gather the information below:

✧ Who is the mayor of your city?

✧ Who is the governor of your state?

✧ Who is president of your country?

✧ Name one U.S. Senator from your state.

✧ Name one U.S. Representative to Congress from your state.

✧ Name one state senator who works in your state capitol.

✧ Name one councilperson who makes laws for your city.

✧ Name one state representative who works in your state capitol.

✧ Name one U.S. Supreme Court justice.

✧ Name one judge in your state's highest court.

✧ ✧ **Vocabulary Words** ✧ ✧

branches of government

enforced

executive

federal

House of Representatives

interpret

judicial

legislative

levels of government

local

repealing

state

United States Senate

LESSON 7

The Age of Responsibility

Objectives

As a result of this lesson, students will be able to:

✧ Recognize reasons why some laws discriminate against young people.

✧ Explain how and why young people were treated much differently in earlier periods in history than they are today.

✧ Analyze and explain at what age a person should be held responsible under the legal system.

Imagine you lived 250 years ago. What did you eat? What did you do for entertainment? What did you wear? Without cars, trains, buses or planes, how did you get from one place to another? How were you treated as a young person?

The following interviews are with two twelve-year-olds. Because few young people hundreds of years ago were given the opportunity to learn to read and write, they could not write their stories. The stories are based on the lives of real people during two different periods in history.

The year is 1725. Matthew is talking about his life.

"I live with my father and mother in the colony of New York. I always do what my father tells me. I know my father treats me as if he owns me, but I wish he would treat me better than the cows. I know the cows are more important, but he treats the cows so much better. My father says that I can't learn to read and write. It wouldn't help me, he said. It would take away from my chores. He says if I give him any trouble, he will throw me out of the house. He has already beat me nearly to death. I know an eight-year-old boy who was thrown out of his house. While on his own, he became hungry and stole some bread. He is now in jail near the stables. I guess I'll stay with my father. What else can I do?"

The year is 1892. Olivia is talking about her life.

"I live with my mother in Massachusetts. I work in a factory day after day, except for Sunday. I work beginning at sunrise until long after dark at the mill. I cut cloth. I am very careful because my friend Susan lost three fingers a few weeks ago. The light is not very good, and she just couldn't see well enough. She has another job now. I get one break for noonday meal. I wish we got to eat more. I'm so hungry. The soup doesn't fill my stomach. I'd love the chance to learn to read. I'd just like to know what the signs in the mill say. But I can't go to school because my mother needs every penny of the money I make to pay for the food and the rent. Last Christmas she had enough to buy me a new hat. I wish life was different. It won't ever be."

What do these two twelve year olds, Olivia and Matthew, have in common?

How are children in the U.S. today different from Olivia and Matthew?

Why are children's lives different today?

How are laws which affect young people different today?

Give some examples of laws that affect young people today.

The following law is an example of a state law or **statute** that affects young people.

294.030. Hours of work for minors.—1. A child under sixteen years of age shall not be employed, permitted or suffered to work at any gainful occupation for more than eight hours in any day nor more than six days or forty hours in any week, nor before the hour of seven o'clock in the morning nor after the hour of ten o'clock in the evening.

2. During a school term a child under sixteen years of age shall not be employed, permitted or suffered to work at any gainful occupation after the hour of seven o'clock in the evening on days immediately preceding days when school is in session; . . .

Why do you think this law was written? How would life for Matthew and Olivia be different if this law had been in existence in 1725 and 1892? How might *your* life be different *without* this law?

Another example of a law that affects young people is the legal driving age.

✧ How old must you be in your state in order to get a driver's license? Do you agree or disagree with this law?

✧ At what age do YOU think you should be able to drive a car in your state? Why?

✧ The law gives you a right at a certain age to drive a car. What responsibilities go with that right?

Some laws **discriminate** against young people simply because of their age. However, because all citizens have constitutional rights, laws must discriminate for fair and good reasons. For example, there are laws that **prohibit** young people from working in certain jobs, such as a pattern cutter or military person.

Under the laws, which of the jobs do you think could be done by a young person 16 or under?

meat packer	welder	elected official
truck driver	computer operator	farmer
mail person	diver	teacher
delivery person	doctor	

For which jobs would the law discriminate against young people for a good reason? For which jobs would the law discriminate unfairly? Can you think of any other jobs that provide examples of how a law discriminates against young people in employment? Provide examples and describe whether you think the law discriminates fairly or unfairly.

Think about each of the laws listed below. Do you think these laws are fair? Explain your answers.

1. People must be 16 to drive a car.

YES, the law is fair because . . .   NO, the law is not fair because . . .

2. People must be 18 years old to serve on juries.

YES, the law is fair because . . .   NO, the law is not fair because . . .

3. People must attend school until they are 16 years old.

YES, the law is fair because . . .   NO, the law is not fair because . . .

4. People under 18 cannot sign a contract.

YES, the law is fair because . . .   NO, the law is not fair because . . .

5. People under 18 may not vote in government elections.

YES, the law is fair because . . .   NO, the law is not fair because . . .

6. People under 16 or 17 may not get married without their parents' consent.

YES, the law is fair because . . .   NO, the law is not fair because . . .

MAKING A DIFFERENCE

With the help of your teacher, organize a school-wide debate on the questions listed on this page and page 53 about laws that affect young people. Each class could select one or more students to represent each side of each question—some to argue that the law is fair; some to argue that it is unfair.

·————————————· E X T R A ·————————————·

Below is a list of laws which apply to young people. These laws may vary from state to state. Research the statutes regarding these laws in your state and learn when each law was passed and, if possible, some of the reasons why it was passed. Using this information, answer the questions that follow.

What age must a young person be in your state in order to legally:

1. Drive a car?

2. Serve on juries?

3. Stop going to school?

4. Sign a contract?

5. Vote in government elections?

6. Get married without their parents' consent?

✦ ✦ **Vocabulary Words** ✦ ✦

discriminate   **prohibit**
minors   **statute**

LESSON 8

Juvenile Court and Adult Court

Objectives

As a result of this lesson, students will be able to:

⋄ Identify and explain three reasons or purposes for the establishment of the juvenile court.

⋄ Compare and contrast the differences and similarities between the juvenile court and the adult criminal court.

The year is 1895. A young man is accused of stealing a loaf of bread. He said, when **arrested**, that he was very hungry. He is found **guilty** of stealing and the court sentences him to jail. He is twelve years old. He arrives at the jail for his three month **sentence** to find that the jail is filled with murderers and thieves. In jail he will be treated as any other prisoner.

What do you think three months in jail would be like for a twelve-year-old boy?

In 1895, any young person over seven years of age who broke the law could be sent to adult court. Young people were treated like adults when they went to court. They could be sentenced to spend time in jail. Some people strongly believed that this was not fair. They thought young people should be treated differently from adults. One man put it this way, "Does clubbing a person make him better? Children need care, not harsh punishment!"

What does the question, "Does clubbing a person make him better?" mean? Why do you think this person wanted a separate court for young people?

In the late 1890s, a small group of people who wanted to change the way the law treated young people met in Chicago. They decided on a plan for establishing a special court for young people. They called young people **juveniles** and worked with lawmakers to set up a special group of laws for juveniles called a **juvenile code.** In 1899, the Illinois legislature adopted the first juvenile code in this country. Since then, juvenile codes have been adopted in each state. Part of the Illinois code says: "Children as far as practicable . . . shall be treated not as criminals but as children in need of aid, encouragement, and guidance."

What do you think "as far as practicable" means? What should the juvenile court do with juveniles who commit horrible **crimes** that affect the lives of others?

The laws and courts for juveniles are there to provide care, protection, and discipline for young people. For example, **neglected** or **abused** children may need both care and protection from the court. Other children who break the law may need to be punished. Some of the purposes of the juvenile court are listed below.

A. A juvenile court makes sure that a juvenile is protected from harm, abuse, and neglect.

B. A juvenile court helps a juvenile change his/her ways.

C. A juvenile court punishes juveniles who break the law.

D. A juvenile court protects society from juveniles who break the law.

Look at these purposes and rank them from "1" (most important), to "4" (least important).

Juvenile Court:	Purpose	Rank
	A:	?
	B:	?
	C:	?
	D:	?

Some of the purposes of adult criminal court are listed below.

A. An adult criminal court makes sure that an adult is treated fairly when he/she comes before the court.

B. An adult criminal court helps an adult change his/her ways.

C. An adult criminal court punishes adults who break the law.

D. An adult criminal court protects society from adults who break the law.

Look at these purposes and rank them from "1" (most important) to "4" (least important).

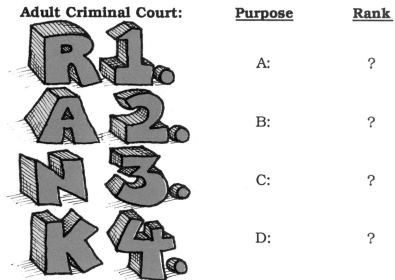

Adult Criminal Court:	__Purpose__	__Rank__
	A:	?
	B:	?
	C:	?
	D:	?

1. Which purpose did you rank most important for juvenile court? Why?

2. Which purpose did you rank most important for adult criminal court? Why?

3. Was your most important purpose for juvenile court the same or different from your most important purpose for adult criminal court? Why?

4. Why did you select your second, third, and fourth choices for juvenile court? For adult criminal court?

The next two pages provide information about the legal differences between juvenile court and adult criminal court. Use this information to investigate the answers to the true-false statements below.

ARE THESE STATEMENTS TRUE OR FALSE?

1. A young person who is 14 can never stand **trial** as an adult.

2. A juvenile court judge can give a juvenile a sentence of life in prison.

3. An adult's criminal record is destroyed once he or she has served time in a **penal** institution.

4. Adult criminal courts have **dispositional hearings.**

5. A juvenile **hearing** is confidential.

There are major differences between the adult criminal courts and the juvenile courts. Here are some of them:

JUVENILE COURT   ADULT COURT

YEARS | 1 2 3 4 5 6 7 8 9 10 11 12 13 14 15 | 16 17 18 | 19 20 21 ——————————➤ | YEARS

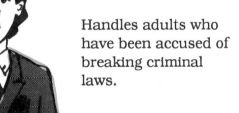

Handles young people who have:
✧ Been abused or neglected by their families.

✧ Broken a special law that applies only to young people, such as being **truant** from school or running away from home.

✧ Broken criminal laws.

Holds a confidential fact-finding hearing (to establish what happened).

Holds a dispositional hearing (to decide what should be done).

Judge could give dispositional alternatives which include **probation**, placement in a foster care home, commitment to a group home or to a minimum or maximum security training school. Juveniles may be ordered to remain in juvenile custody for an indeterminate period, and in some **jurisdictions**, until age 21.

Handles adults who have been accused of breaking criminal laws.

Holds a public trial.

Gives a sentence or penalty. Punishment can be a fine, probation, or imprisonment in a city jail, a state or federal prison.

JUVENILE COURT   ADULT COURT

YEARS | 1 2 3 4 5 6 7 8 9 10 11 12 13 14 15 | 16 17 18 | 19 20 21 ————————→ | YEARS

Most severe penalty: about a two-year term in a maximum security state institution for juveniles. But, a young person may be **certified** as an adult for committing a particular crime. When this happens the juvenile has to go through the adult court process.

Both attorneys—the **prosecuting attorney** and the **defense attorney**—work for the best interest of the young person and of society.

The juvenile court judge decides the facts of the case and the disposition.

A young person found to be **delinquent** receives a record. In most instances, this information is sealed when the juvenile becomes an adult. However, a record of **offenses** committed remains.

Most severe penalty: life in prison or (in some states) **capital punishment**.

The prosecuting attorney represents the public and tries to prove that a crime was committed by the defendant. The defense attorney represents the defendant and tries to prove that he/she is not guilty.

Either a jury or a judge without a jury decides the facts of the case and the sentence.

An adult convicted of a crime has a criminal record for a lifetime.

There are many differences between the juvenile court and adult criminal court. One difference is the words that are used to describe what happens in each court. Look carefully at the sentences below. Why is each capitalized term used in juvenile court different from the related term for adult criminal court? Review the purposes of each court and identify which purpose or purposes you think each term represents.

- A juvenile is TAKEN INTO CUSTODY; an adult is ARRESTED.

- A juvenile commits an OFFENSE; an adult commits a CRIME.

- A juvenile has a HEARING; an adult has a TRIAL.

- A juvenile is found DELINQUENT; an adult is found GUILTY.

- A juvenile receives a DISPOSITION; an adult receives a SENTENCE.

The words are important for understanding the reasons for the existence of juvenile court. The next lesson will help you to learn more about how the juvenile court actually works and what happens when a juvenile is **taken into custody.**

There are many people—parents and other adults, as well as young people like you—who want to know more about how the juvenile justice system works. They need factual information concerning the juvenile court. Your class could sponsor a program for the school parents' association meeting to provide some information on the juvenile court.

You could invite a judge of the juvenile court in your community or a court social worker or a counselor to be guest speaker at the parents' association meeting. The class could submit to the speaker a list of several questions which you, as a group, decide are the most important. This list should be sent to the speaker at least a week before the date of the meeting. Such a list would help the speaker know exactly which aspects of the court's work your group wants to know about.

You will have to work closely with the program chairperson or president of the parents' association in carefully planning the program for the meeting. You may want to help distribute their meeting announcement. The speaker should know how much time he/she has on the program. He/she should also be asked to plan on spending time to answer questions from the audience.

Of course the entire class should attend the meeting. Perhaps the parents' association would like some members of the class to act as hosts and hostesses for the meeting. By getting involved, you will learn more about the juvenile court. You will also show the school staff and your parents that you are interested and concerned.

· E X T R A ·

Review the information on pages 61-62. Use the library or contact the juvenile court to seek answers to the following questions:

✧ At what age may a juvenile be certified to stand trial as an adult in your state?

✧ At what age may juveniles be certified in states near your state?

✧ What is your state's juvenile court policy regarding sealing juvenile records? Under what circumstances may a juvenile's record be opened for examination?

Report your answers to the teacher and class. You may wish to write an article for your school or local newspaper describing the answers to the above questions.

✧ ✧ Vocabulary Words ✧ ✧

abused

arrested

capital punishment

certified

crimes

defense attorney

delinquent

dispositional hearing

guilty

hearing

jurisdiction

juveniles

juvenile code

neglected

offenses

penal

probation

prosecuting attorney

sentence

taken into custody

trial

truant

LESSON 9

Juvenile Rights to Due Process: The Case of Gerald Gault

Objectives

As a result of this lesson, students will be able to:

✧ Explain what the constitutional right to due process means for juveniles.

✧ Identify specific due process rights for juveniles who are taken into custody.

Today, young people under a certain age (it varies from state to state) are by law considered juveniles. Juvenile courts have been set up to handle their cases. The juvenile court must follow certain steps, or a process, in reaching a decision about a juvenile. *How* the decision is reached is in many ways as important as *what* the decision is. Being treated fairly has to do not only with what decision is made about you, but also how that decision is made.

Law enforcement officers, lawyers and other juvenile specialists assist judges in reaching a decision about the juvenile. In this process certain rules of law are applied in arriving at a decision. A juvenile who is accused of committing an offense becomes involved in the juvenile court process. There are certain rules of law that must be followed as part of this legal process to **safeguard** the juvenile's right to get fair treatment.

The **fourteenth amendment** to the United States Constitution says that all people have the right to be treated fairly in a legal procedure. This is called "**due process** of law."

The fourteenth amendment states in part:

> ". . . nor shall any state deprive any person of life, liberty, or property without due process of law."

Due process means:

✧ Looking at the facts that can be proven, rather than making judgments on something you hear.

✧ Having an attorney represent you.

✧ Having all sides of a story brought out.

✧ Being told of the offense you are charged with.

✧ Reasonable punishment to fit the crime.

. . . And it has come to mean much more. Courts continue to interpret the U.S. Constitution and laws, and lawmakers continue to make new laws concerning what fair treatment (due process) means.

Juveniles did not always have these due process rights. For a long time these safeguards applied only to adult criminal trials. The juvenile court started with the idea that young people did not need the same safeguards that an adult in a criminal case would need. Juvenile court had very informal hearings. It was thought that juveniles would be better off to have an informal hearing rather than a formal legal procedure. Then in 1967 the United States Supreme Court was asked to make a decision regarding the rights of juveniles in the case of a fifteen-year-old boy from Arizona named Gerald Gault.

The following two pages describe Gerald's story.

June 8

June 9

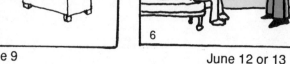

June 12 or 13

June 15th
Hearing

Make a list of the things that happened or did not happen during this legal procedure that you think made the process unfair. Read the following questions to help you in developing your list. Explain why you think these things were unfair.

1. When were Gerald's parents notified?

2. Did Gerald have a lawyer present at his hearing? Explain your answer.

3. What was Gerald told that he was being charged with?

4. Was there a record of the hearing?

5. Where was Mrs. Cook during the hearing?

6. Did Gerald know that anything he said could be used against him? Explain your answer.

7. Was Gerald's punishment reasonable? Why or why not?

8. If Gerald was an adult would he have received such a severe punishment? Why or why not?

Something did happen in the case of Gerald Gault. After he went to the State Training School, his parents went to a lawyer and explained everything that had happened to Gerald. The lawyer agreed that if what the Gaults said was true, Gerald had not been given fair treatment. He had been denied "due process of law."

Since Arizona law at that time did not allow cases involving juveniles to be taken to a higher court, the lawyer asked the state court in Arizona for a **writ of habeas corpus** (a writ of habeas corpus is a procedure by which people already in prison can have the legality of their imprisonment reviewed in a higher court). He argued that the Juvenile Code of Arizona went against the due process clause of the fifth and fourteenth amendment of the U.S. Constitution. The case was finally heard by the United States Supreme Court. The Supreme Court ruled in favor of Gerald Gault.

Before 1967 young people were not given the due process rights listed below. What happened to Gerald Gault could have happened to other young people.

After 1967 courts and police officers dealing with juveniles must follow the decision made by the Supreme Court in Gerald Gault's case. They have to make sure that young persons coming to the juvenile court are protected by the due process safeguards. These safeguards have been developed since 1967. The list below describes these safeguards.

In the Gault case the Supreme Court ruled that juveniles who are accused of offenses for which they could be sent to an institution must have the following rights:

1. **RIGHT TO NOTICE OF CHARGES:** Being told exactly what you are accused of long enough in advance of your hearing to be able to prepare your case.

2. **RIGHT TO COUNSEL:** Being told you have a right to a lawyer, that if you don't have enough money to pay, the court must appoint a lawyer for you.

3. **RIGHT TO CONFRONTATION AND CROSS-EXAMINATION:** Being able to hear the **testimony** of the witnesses and of your accusers. Testimony is the information a witness gives under oath. Cross-examination means that the accused or the lawyer for the accused has the chance to ask the witness questions.

4. **PRIVILEGE AGAINST SELF-INCRIMINATION:** Being told you have a right to remain silent because anything you say might be used against you.

In later cases the courts have since ruled that an accused juvenile must have the right to:

5. **A TRANSCRIPT OF THE PROCEEDINGS:** Having the official record of the proceedings of a trial or hearing. This is a word-for-word record of the proceedings.

6. **AN APPELLATE REVIEW:** Having the right to ask to have your case heard by a higher court if you wish to have the decision reached in the first hearing reversed.

Where are these rights supported in the U.S. Constitution? Review the Bill of Rights to the U.S. Constitution provided in the back of your book. Try to match the rights listed above with the appropriate amendment to the U.S. Constitution.

		Amendment
1.	Notice of Charges	?
2.	Counsel	?
3.	Confrontation and cross-examination	?
4.	Self-incrimination	?
5.	Transcript	?
6.	Appellate review	?

Below is a sample form that one juvenile court uses to assure that a juvenile who is in the court system knows his or her rights at the court. Read through the form and see if you can identify the rights from the Gault case. Why do you think each right is important?

JUVENILE DIVISION—CIRCUIT COURT
NOTICE UPON ADMISSION TO THE DETENTION FACILITY

I, _____, born _____, have been fully advised that I am being detained for: _____ and have been fully advised of the following rights which exist under the law on this _____ day of _____, 19 _____, by _____ a worker acting for the Juvenile Court. I have been specifically informed that:

1. I have the right to remain silent. This means that I do not have to answer any questions or make any statements unless I wish to do so. If I decide to make a statement, I have the right to stop talking at any time.

2. I have the right to consult with and be represented by an attorney. If I wish, I will be given the opportunity to telephone an attorney. If I am unable to hire an attorney, the Court will appoint one to represent me without cost. The Public Defender is available to represent me at this time. The Public Defender will be contacted for me whenever I ask that the Public Defender be contacted.

3. I have the right to a Detention Hearing before the Juvenile Court to determine whether detention is necessary. The Detention Hearing will be held within three days, excluding Saturdays, Sundays and holidays. At the Detention Hearing I may be represented by an attorney.

4. When placed in detention, I may immediately make a telephone call to my parent(s) and my attorney. While in detention, I may make further telephone calls to my parent(s) and my attorney at reasonable times.

5. When admitted to the detention facility, my parent(s) and my attorney may visit me. The first visit may be made at any time. After the first visit, my parent(s) may visit me during the visiting hours, and my attorney may visit at any reasonable time.

6. If I refuse to see my parent(s), my parent(s) may visit me only if authorized by the Juvenile Judge or the Juvenile Officer.

7. No person other than my parent(s), attorney, Juvenile Officer or member of the Juvenile Court staff may interview or question me in detention unless authorized by the Juvenile Judge or authorized Juvenile Officer, or unless agreed to by my attorney, or unless my attorney is present.

8. If I am fourteen years of age or older and am accused of committing an act which would have been a felony if committed by an adult or which is a violation of a traffic law, the Court may have me prosecuted as an adult. In such a case, anything I say may be used against me in a criminal proceeding.

I understand these rights. _____
Juvenile

The case of Gerald Gault made important changes in the legal process used to handle young people who came before the juvenile courts. The juvenile court is still undergoing changes. It may be very different six years from now. How it changes depends upon people—people who care enough to learn about the court and to work for improvement. There is much discussion today about the juvenile court as shown in the following headlines.

TOUGHER COURTS NEEDED FOR JUVENILES

High Court May Consider Juvenile Rights

Youth Violence: More To It Than Headlines Say

STATE'S ATTORNEY SEEKS TO TRY YOUTH AS ADULT FOR MURDER

People are discussing the purposes of the juvenile court and how it works for the 1990s. Think about the questions on the juvenile court that follow:

Do you think it really helps young people? Why or why not?
Is it more fair to young people than an adult court? Why or why not?
Is it fair to the rest of society? Why or why not?

Activity #1

Many people have never heard of the Gault case and don't really know what constitutional rights were involved. As a class you might write a script for a skit about the Gault case. You could act out the story from start to finish. If you need more facts for your story, ask a law student, a lawyer, or someone who knows how to use a law library to find the case. You can follow the actual story fact-by-fact as it appears in the reported case.

Do your presentation for an audience—perhaps another class or a parent group. You might even make a videotape of the story.

Activity #2

Draw your own cartoon story of the case of Gerald Gault as it might happen today. Be certain to include the specific rights of the young person that the court must uphold. Share your stories with other classes in your school. One way of organizing your story is shown below.

The Case Of Gerald Gault As It Might Have Happened After The 1967 Supreme Court Decision According To _____

(your name)

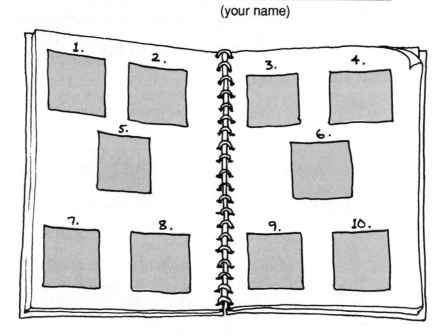

•———————————————— E X T R A •————————————————•

Activity #1

Use a law library and research other cases since the Gault case in which the U.S. Supreme Court has established a position on due process rights for juveniles.

Activity #2

Contact your juvenile court to see if they have a form that explains the rights of juveniles taken into custody, and if not, how they communicate this information to juveniles.

✧ ✧ **Vocabulary Words** ✧ ✧

due process	**safeguard**
fourteenth amendment	**self-incrimination**
right to confrontation	**testimony**
right to cross-examination	**writ of habeas corpus**

LESSON 10

The Juvenile Court Process

Objectives

As a result of this lesson, students will be able to:

✧ Recognize and explain the basic steps involved in the juvenile court process.

✧ Analyze the reasons why there is discretion in the juvenile court system in deciding what should happen to the juvenile.

✧ Explain that juveniles who become a part of the juvenile court process remain under the court's jurisdiction until released.

As you have learned, juveniles have rights and responsibilities. The constitutional rights of juveniles must be respected by law enforcement officials. A police officer must follow certain legally prescribed steps when taking a juvenile into **custody.** At each step of this process, the authorities (police, deputy juvenile officers, judge, commissioner, or hearing officers) can exercise their **discretion** and release you back to your parents or to some other court-approved custodian.

You learned in Lesson 9 that juveniles have a right to be treated fairly under the law when they enter the juvenile court system. They have the right to due process. This lesson takes you through a juvenile court process. The due process steps apply to juvenile cases anywhere in the United States. However, the specific procedure for handling juveniles may vary depending upon the locality.

YOU BE THE JUDGE

There are a variety of reasons a juvenile might be taken into custody by the police or juvenile officers. In order to make a determination about whether or not a juvenile should be released or should remain under the jurisdiction of the court, the authorities take a number of things into account including:

✧ Whether or not the juvenile is a threat to himself or herself.

✧ Whether or not the juvenile is a threat to others.

✧ Whether or not the juvenile is likely to run away prior to any scheduled court hearing.

✧ The juvenile's age.

✧ The offense for which the juvenile is being held.

✧ The juvenile's past history.

✧ The juvenile's school record.

✧ Where and with whom the juvenile is currently living.

Review the four juvenile cases on the next page. Determine whether or not you believe the juvenile should be released at Step 1 of the four steps in the court process described on the next pages. Try to make a judgment based on the information you have, just as the court officials would do. In some cases you may feel you need more information. Write down whatever you would want answered on a sheet of paper and keep a record of this information. Keep in mind, the juvenile's past record with the juvenile court may give some indication as to the potential threat a person may be to him or herself, or to others.

In order to make this activity real to you, use your imagination and try to think of an actual person for each of the following four juveniles.

	Age	Offense	Past Court History	Lives
Juvenile A (male)	10	Burglary (In daytime— no one home)	(1) Curfew violation (2) Truancy	With Grand- parents
Juvenile B (male)	14	Purse snatching	(1) Burglary (2) Burglary	In Court Group Home
Juvenile C (female)	13	Curfew violation	(1) **Incorrigible**	With Parents
Juvenile D (female)	12	Runaway	(1) Runaway (2) Runaway	With Parents

STEPS IN THE JUVENILE COURT PROCESS

There are four basic steps in the process whereby juveniles are taken into the justice system and ultimately released from it. Juveniles who enter the system do not necessarily go through all the steps. For example, a juvenile who is taken into custody by the police as a suspected thief may be released after an initial hearing. A brief description of the steps in the overall process and the different possible outcomes at each step are summarized below and on the following pages.

Step 1: The Juvenile Is Taken Into Custody

In order for the police to take a juvenile into custody, they usually need "**probable cause**." Probable cause is a reasonable belief that a crime has been committed and that the person being taken into custody is the one who committed the crime. In some jurisdictions police are permitted to take a juvenile into custody if the police believe the juvenile is "in need of supervision," or if they believe the juvenile is "endangered." In these cases, **reasonable suspicion** is sufficient for the police to take the juvenile into custody.

Police pick up the juvenile and take him or her either to the police station, or directly to juvenile court. At either place they can ask the juvenile his or her name, address, and age and search the juvenile for any concealed weapons. The juvenile is allowed to call his or her parents. The alleged offense cannot be discussed with the juvenile unless there is a deputy juvenile officer there to read the juvenile his or her rights. What do you think are some basic rights a person is entitled to whenever he or she is arrested or taken into custody?

The juvenile is often questioned by a juvenile court intake officer. The officer may choose to release the juvenile at this point if there isn't enough evidence to keep him or her in custody. In many states, the officer will notify the juvenile's parents soon after the juvenile is in custody. Depending upon the seriousness of the offense and the juvenile's history, the intake officer may allow him or her to return home in the custody of his or her parents until the court date. Remember, at this stage of the process, the juvenile is only *accused* of committing a **delinquent act,** not yet guilty of anything.

Should the intake officer be allowed to lock up any juvenile at this stage of the process? Why or why not?

If the offense is serious enough, the juvenile will not be released but will be assigned to a **detention center.** In this case, the juvenile's clothes are exchanged for court-provided clothes. He or she is told to take a shower and is put in confinement. If time permits, more investigation is done. The next morning, or in a reasonably short period of time, the deputy juvenile officer presents the facts he or she has gathered to the chief juvenile officer. Together they decide whether or not to hold the juvenile until a detention hearing.

YOU BE THE **JUDGE**

What would you do about the juveniles from page 78 based on the information you have so far? Would you release at Step 1 after intake?

	Yes	No	Why
Juvenile A:	?	?	?
Juvenile B:	?	?	?
Juvenile C:	?	?	?
Juvenile D:	?	?	?

Step 2: The Preliminary Hearing

A detention or **preliminary hearing** is held:

◇ To decide whether or not the court will take custody of the juvenile.

◇ To decide whether or not the juvenile will be kept in detention or be released to the parents. If the juvenile judge decides to order the juvenile to be held in detention, the judge usually orders one of the following:

- Keep the juvenile in secure detention;
- Send the juvenile to a community-based group home or temporary foster home;
- Transfer the juvenile to a shelter care center or psychiatric clinic if the judge believes it is in the best interests of the juvenile.

In most jurisdictions, a juvenile has a right to be represented by a lawyer at the detention hearing, and the parents and juvenile should be notified of this right. If they cannot afford a lawyer, one will be appointed by the court.

In most jurisdictions, the detention hearing is held promptly, usually within 48 to 96 hours of the juvenile being taken into custody. Under the Federal Juvenile Delinquency Act, a juvenile in custody may not be detained for longer than a reasonable period of time before being brought before a hearing judge.

In many states a juvenile is asked to admit whether the charges are true or false at this hearing. A juvenile should have a lawyer present at this hearing. The lawyer checks the facts and makes sure all procedures are properly followed.

Prior to this hearing, a juvenile court counselor talks with the juvenile and his or her parent to learn about the juvenile's life at school and at home. The juvenile counselor's responsibility is to learn the special circumstances and background of each juvenile. The counselor must also review the different places where the juvenile might be sent. Based on knowledge of the juvenile and of the available places for juveniles, the counselor makes a recommendation to the judge. The counselor writes a report and presents it to the judge before the hearing.

YOU BE THE COUNSELOR

Refer to the juveniles on page 78. Imagine if you were the counselor assigned to talk with each juvenile. What questions would you ask? How would those questions help you do your job as counselor? Your teacher may have you role play. You play the role of counselor and another student plays one of the juveniles, like Juvenile B. You ask him or her questions, and based on the answers, you make a recommendation to the judge.

If a juvenile does not admit committing the offense (pleads not delinquent), the juvenile court lawyer must prepare his or her case for the **adjudicatory** (fact-finding) **hearing** by trying to put together facts to prove the juvenile committed the offense.

If a juvenile does admit committing the offense (pleads delinquent to the charges) at this hearing, a dispositional hearing will be held, at which the court will decide what to do with the juvenile.

Step 3: The Adjudicatory Hearing

The adjudicatory hearing is the juvenile court's version of an adult criminal trial. An adjudicatory hearing is held:

✧ To find the facts; to decide whether or not the juvenile committed the offense(s) of which he or she stands accused.

A juvenile has a right to have a lawyer present. In most jurisdictions, the court insists that the juvenile be represented by an attorney during this hearing.

Why do you think it is so important for a juvenile to have an attorney during the adjudicatory hearing?

Under the Federal Juvenile Delinquency Act, a juvenile must have an opportunity for an adjudicatory hearing within 30 days after being taken into custody. In most cases, if a juvenile is being held in detention, the adjudicatory hearing occurs even quicker. This right to a "speedy trial" is protected by the sixth amendment of the United States Constitution.

At the adjudicatory hearing, an attorney for the juvenile court presents evidence to the judge about why it is believed that the juvenile is delinquent. The juvenile's lawyer presents evidence about why he or she is innocent. Sometimes others such as the arresting police officers testify. Juveniles may also testify on their own behalf, but the United States Constitution protects them from having to testify if they do not want to.

At the conclusion of all the evidence, the judge, in most cases, must decide whether the juvenile is delinquent or not delinquent **beyond a reasonable doubt.** In a few states, juveniles are permitted to request jury trials. In adult criminal cases, a defendant has a constitutional right to have a jury make this decision.

If the juvenile is found not delinquent, the process ends and he or she is released. If the juvenile is found delinquent, the process continues to a third hearing, called the dispositional hearing.

If the juvenile believes he or she did not receive fair treatment or the judge made an error, then the juvenile, in many jurisdictions, may **appeal** the decision.

YOU BE THE
JUDGE

If you were the judge, what evidence would you want to have presented in the case in order to help you reach a finding (see the columns below)?

	Evidence from Juvenile Court Attorney	Evidence from Defense Attorney	Why do you think this evidence is important?
Juvenile A:	?	?	?
Juvenile B:	?	?	?
Juvenile C:	?	?	?
Juvenile D:	?	?	?

Step 4: The Dispositional Hearing

The dispositional hearing is held:

✧ To decide what will be done with the delinquent juvenile.

A judge is often influenced in making a decision about what to do with a juvenile by the recommendation of the social worker or juvenile counselor who has worked with the juvenile. A juvenile has a right to have a lawyer present for the dispositional hearing.

This hearing is usually held immediately after the adjudicatory hearing. Here the judge must decide what to do about the juvenile. The judge must try to balance the need to help the juvenile straighten out his or her behavior against the need to protect society from future delinquent acts which the juvenile might commit. The juvenile court judge has several options. available for dealing with the juvenile's actions. The judge reviews the background social investigation which the juvenile court counselor had prepared earlier. The judge will also listen to the juvenile's parents, teachers, and other persons who may have information about how to best deal with the juvenile. After the judge makes a dispositional decision, the juvenile court process follows up on the decision.

During the entire process, the juvenile court attempts to protect the juvenile's identity and right to privacy. At the close of the process, all court and police records are to be kept secret from the public. If the news media (for example, newspapers, radio, or television) lawfully obtains information about a juvenile in custody, then the media may report that information. However, most newspapers and television stations do not reveal this information as long as the person is still under juvenile, and not adult, jurisdiction.

Why do you think there are laws keeping this information secret? Why do you think most news media do not reveal the identity of juveniles in custody?

In most states, young people have the right to appeal decisions made by the juvenile court. The procedures are different from state to state.

At this point, you probably don't have enough information to make a decision about the disposition of these juveniles. What additional information would you need to make a fair decision?

The chart on the next page may help you to review the different steps in the juvenile court process.

Typical Juvenile Court Process

Taken into custody

Released at police station

Referred to → Juvenile division of court

Released

Pretrial detention home

Custody of parents

Prosecuting attorney

Serious crimes may be referred to adult court

Case dropped

Pretrial detention (juvenile institution)

Custody of parents (home)

Initial hearing

Adjudicatory hearing

Disposition hearing

Appeal

Juvenile institution

Halfway house or foster home

Probation (home)

You might do a brochure or a videotape about the juvenile court process where you live. You could include several different cases to show the many kinds of problems the juvenile court handles.

You might work with a group in your community that is particularly interested in juveniles, a juvenile police officer, or a counselor. They can assist you in working with your teacher to contact your juvenile court judge to ask his or her permission and cooperation in your project. Perhaps you could get permission to film your production in places in the juvenile court if you are doing a video tape. You will also need assistance in making certain your presentation of the process is accurate in your video or brochure.

You could share your video or brochure with other classes, your school's parent organization, other community groups and of course the court itself.

· E X T R A ·

You could research the steps in your own community's juvenile court process and prepare a chart similar to the one on page 86.

✧ ✧ Vocabulary Words ✧ ✧

adjudicatory hearing
appeal
beyond a reasonable doubt
custody
delinquent act
detention center

discretion
incorrigible
preliminary hearing
probable cause
reasonable suspicion

LESSON 11

A Juvenile Court Hearing

Objectives

As a result of this lesson, students will be able to:

✧ Explain the different types of child welfare cases which require juvenile court intervention, the manner in which they are brought to the attention of the court, and the actual in-court procedures used to decide and resolve these matters.

✧ Identify and explain the job responsibilities of people involved in a juvenile hearing.

In Lesson 10, the procedures and steps for juvenile delinquency cases coming before the juvenile court were discussed. However, delinquency cases are only one part of the juvenile court's work. Of equal importance is the power of the court to perform the function of "**parens patriae**" for the state. "Parens patriae" are Latin words which mean "parent of the country." In the U.S., this term has come to mean the state's role as the protector of children. Each state has laws to protect the physical, mental, and emotional health and welfare of children. These **child welfare** laws are slightly different in each state, but they usually fall into two areas:

1. **CHILD ABUSE** **Child abuse** is defined generally in terms of actions taken by a child's parent or guardian which actively and intentionally hurt the child. A parent's beating of a five-year-old child with an iron rod is an example of physical abuse. There is often a fine line between legitimate physical discipline of a child and child abuse.

   What might be an example of physical discipline which is not child abuse?

   A parent's locking a child in a dark closet for 24 hours at a time is another example. This treatment can leave emotional scars, and is considered psychological abuse. What might be an example of parental discipline which is not psychological abuse?

2. **NEGLECT** **Neglect** is generally defined as an action by a parent or guardian which is thoughtless or selfish and which places the child in a dangerous situation. A parent leaving a two-year-old alone in an apartment for eight hours while the parent visits some friends may be an example of neglect. A parent's refusal to seek medical care for a sick child because it is a distance to the hospital is another example. Failure to provide proper schooling is considered educational neglect and is a violation of the law. A parent who fails to provide a safe and adequate living environment for a child is also committing neglect. If a parent cannot afford adequate housing, then the parent should seek help. It is the responsibility of a parent or guardian to provide for the welfare of a child by making it possible for his or her child to live in a safe and healthy environment.

FROM THE COMMUNITY TO THE COURTS

Child abuse and neglect cases can come to the attention of the juvenile court in many different ways. Every state now has laws establishing a way (like a hotline number) that persons can alert the authorities if they believe a child is being harmed by his or her parents or by his or her living conditions. Most states also require by law that persons such as teachers and doctors report any case where they suspect a child's welfare may be in danger. Once such a call or report is received, an investigation into the case will immediately begin. In some cases, the report of abuse or neglect may be completely untrue.

What are some reasons why someone would make a false report?

If there does appear to be some danger to the child's welfare, the police or other authorities may immediately remove the child from his or her family and place the child in temporary emergency **foster care.**

If the investigating agency finds evidence of abuse and neglect, the agency has several alternatives to recommend, such as:

✧ Filing a petition in the appropriate court, asking the court to declare the child abused and/or neglected.

✧ Encourage the parents to participate in an educational or counseling program for parents (the agency may inform the parents that they may have to go to court for abuse and neglect charges if they do not participate in this program).

✧ Encourage the parents to accept voluntary help.

✧ Refer the family and/or child to a community service or family agency for assistance.

Many cases are referred to the appropriate court for action.

Most states now provide that a preliminary hearing be held by the juvenile or family court to determine if the child needs to be removed from the home until the adjudicatory hearing. In some jurisdictions, child abuse and neglect cases are heard in family court.

THE HEARING

Juvenile courts have two hearings to handle child abuse and neglect cases. The first hearing is the adjudicatory, or fact-finding, hearing. The lawyers present **evidence** and ask the witnesses questions to bring the facts of the case before the court. The judge makes a decision based on the **clear and convincing evidence**. If the judge decides it is a case of child abuse or neglect, then the court has the power to do something about it.

The second hearing is the dispositional hearing. At this hearing the court decides what should be done. Usually a social worker who has studied the possible alternatives makes a recommendation to the judge. The lawyers can argue about this recommendation if they don't think it is fair or accurate. The judge makes the final decision.

Often there is another lawyer called the **guardian ad litem.** This lawyer is appointed by the court to protect the child's interest during the case. "Ad litem" means "at the trial" or "for the suit." This lawyer's job is to make sure that what the court decides to do is in the best interest of the child. A guardian ad litem is not always an attorney (see page 100 for further details about the guardian ad litem).

If the court does not believe there is any real and immediate threat to the child, it may order that the child be returned home until the adjudicatory hearing. If it believes such a threat does exist, it will order that the child remain in temporary emergency foster care.

Read this account of how a juvenile court handled the case of Robbie and Danny Lloyd. Robbie and Danny's family may have a problem where the appropriate court needs to get involved because the boys are possibly being abused or neglected.

You can decide this case by conducting a mock hearing.

THE CASE OF ROBBIE AND DANNY LLOYD ———

Jan. 4

Child Abuse Hot Line Service receives call of possible child abuse concerning Robbie (age 10) and Danny Lloyd (age 2). A neighbor reports Robbie has asked her for food for himself and his little brother, Danny. The neighbor is concerned because she has seen the boys' mother leave the children home alone and stay away several hours. The neighbor reports Robbie looks skinny and sick; and his hair, face, hands, and clothes are dirty. A Child Abuse Hot Line volunteer reports this call to Division of Family Services.

Jan. 6

A social worker from Division of Family Services goes to the Lloyds' home. He finds no food in the home, heating only with space heaters, and no phone. Mrs. Lloyd says she only left the boys home alone once or twice when she has been looking for a job. She said the boys' grandmother was supposed to babysit but never showed up. She says she brings in food every day for the boys and herself. The social worker asks Mrs. Lloyd if there is any way that he could help. Mrs. Lloyd says no. The social worker warns her not to leave her boys alone at home any more.

Feb. 12

Child Abuse Hot Line Service receives another telephone call from the neighbor concerning Robbie and Danny Lloyd. Robbie has been over to ask for food again at 9 o'clock at night. The neighbor said that Danny was home alone when Robbie came home from school and that his mother has not come back since leaving the home earlier in the afternoon.

Feb. 14

The social worker talks to Mrs. Lloyd. He finds out Mrs. Lloyd has not had steady work for the past few months. The social worker notices scars on Robbie's legs. Robbie said his mother beat him with a strap. Mrs. Lloyd said she does whip him when he misbehaves.

Feb. 15

The social worker reports possible case of child abuse and neglect to juvenile court. Based upon this information, the juvenile court investigates the case further. The juvenile court attorney decides to proceed on the case and draws up a petition which states the reasons why it is believed that the Lloyd family has problems where the juvenile court must become involved.

In The Circuit Court Of Jackson County, Missouri
Juvenile Division
Kansas City, Missouri 64108
625 E. 26th Street

PETITION

IN THE INTEREST OF:

Robert Lloyd/Daniel Lloyd   PETITION NO.   64807

NAME

1042 Woodacre   FILE NO.   39288

ADDRESS

4-21-80/1-31-88

BIRTHDATE

The parents or legal guardian of the child/children are:

father deceased   /   Mary Lloyd

    (Father)   (Mother)

and they reside at:

1042 Woodacre

The person having legal custody of the child/children is:

Mother

Comes now the Juvenile Officer, within and for Jackson County, Missouri, and alleges that the child is within Jackson County, Missouri, and is in need of the care, treatment and services of the court because:

The environment of Robbie Lloyd and Danny Lloyd is harmful to their own welfare because the person legally responsible for their proper care and supervision fails or is unable to properly provide such, in that:

    Robbie and Danny are left alone at home continually for several hours at a time

    there is unsafe heating in their apartment

    Robbie shows scars resulting from being whipped with a strap

    Mrs. Lloyd does not feed and take care of the boys properly

Petitioner states that this is a physically, psychologically, and emotionally harmful environment for the children to live in.

WHEREFORE, petitioner prays the court to sustain this petition and to order appropriate supervision, care, examination, treatment, detention, placement, commitment, change of custody, or other disposition of said child as provided under provisions of chapter 211. R.S. Mo as amended.

A copy of the foregoing petition mailed/delivered this 15th day of Feb. 19 90 to Appointed Attorney for said child.

Barry Horwitz

Juvenile Officer of Jackson County, Missouri

By _____

_____   DEPUTY

JUVENILE OFFICER

Feb. 16

The social worker, accompanied by a police officer, takes Robbie and Danny from their home and places them in emergency foster care.

Feb. 19

A detention hearing is held. The juvenile court attorney presents evidence explaining why Robbie and Danny should not be released to Mrs. Lloyd. Mrs. Lloyd is present, but is not represented by an attorney. The judge is informed that she is entitled to have an attorney represent her, and if she is unable to afford an attorney, the court will appoint someone to represent her in this case. Mrs. Lloyd says she loves Robbie and Danny and wants them back home with her. The judge decides not to release Robbie and Danny at this time. Mrs. Lloyd is given notice of the time and place for the adjudicatory and possible dispositional hearing.

In The Circuit Court Of Jackson County, Missouri
Juvenile Division

Kansas City, Missouri 64108

625 E. 26th Street

NOTICE TO PARENT/GUARDIAN, CHILD
OF COURT HEARING

Robert & Daniel Lloyd   PETITION NO.   64807

IN THE INTEREST OF

1042 Woodacre   FILE NO.   39288

ADDRESS

4-21-80/1-31-88

BIRTHDATE

Enclosed is a copy of the Petition/Motion to Modify filed in the interest of the above named child(ren). If you have obtained an attorney to represent your child(ren), I would appreciate being notified as to his or her name. Thank you for your co-operation in this matter.

The Court Hearing is set for:

DAY: Monday

DATE: March 19, 1990

TIME: 9:00 a.m.

Sincerely,

Administrative Supervisor

FORM 044-COR
3-5M-7/76

THE HEARING

Your class can plan to conduct a court hearing for the case of Robbie and Danny Lloyd. For your hearing you will need people to take the roles of:

1. Juvenile court attorney

2. Defense attorney

3. Judge

4. **Court reporter**

5. **Bailiff**

6. **Clerk**

7. Guardian ad litem

8. Robbie Lloyd, juvenile (witness for juvenile court attorney)

9. Mr. Barry Horwitz, social worker (witness for juvenile court attorney)

10. Mrs. Mary Lloyd, mother (witness for defense attorney)

11. Mrs. Martha Cooper, grandmother (witness for defense attorney)

    If possible, try to arrange your classroom to resemble the typical courtroom set up illustrated below.

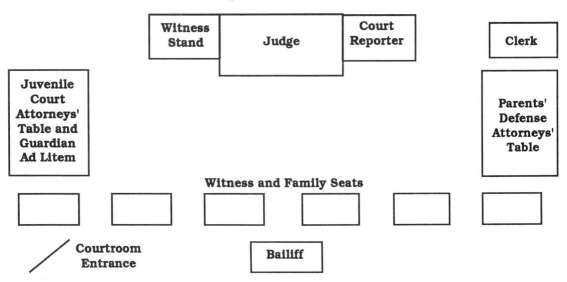

To Prepare for the Hearing

Read through the following descriptions for the hearing. After reading what is expected of each person, decide who will play each role at your hearing.

1. **Juvenile Court Attorney** Two students may wish to help play this role. One student can be the attorney and one can be the attorney's assistant.

   The juvenile court attorney represents the state (similar to a prosecuting attorney in adult criminal court.) The juvenile court attorney's job is to prove with "clear and convincing evidence" that Robbie and Danny's situation is harmful to them. You must prove that, for the reasons stated in the petition, the environment Robbie and Danny live in is harmful to their welfare. Your job is to prove that the children are in fact being abused and neglected.

   To prepare for the hearing, talk with the social worker and Robbie. Make sure you understand what their stories are. Think about the questions you plan to ask them during the hearing. Also think about the questions you may wish to ask the other witnesses. Ask the judge to explain the types of questions you are not allowed to ask (page 98).

   At the hearing you will call the social worker to the witness stand first. Then you will call Robbie to the stand.

· · · · **Facts to Know** · · · ·

"Clear and convincing evidence" is a legal term describing a certain degree of proof needed to make a decision (in other words, how much evidence, how many facts do you have to establish in order to show that the condition—abuse or neglect—exists). The juvenile court attorney has to prove only that there is strong evidence that abuse happened. It is not as strict a standard as "proof beyond a reasonable doubt" which is required in criminal trials.

2. **Defense Attorney** (for Mrs. Lloyd) One student can be the defense attorney and one student can be the attorney's assistant.

   In most jurisdictions, parents accused of abusing and/or neglecting their children are entitled to be represented by a defense attorney. In most jurisdictions, an attorney will be appointed for the parents if they are unable to afford an attorney. Your job is to represent Mrs. Lloyd and to prove that Mrs. Lloyd is taking care of her children, and that the juvenile court has no right to step in and tell Mrs. Lloyd what to do with her children. At the hearing you should try to bring out information that is favorable to Mrs. Lloyd such as:

   ✧ Mrs. Lloyd did not leave her boys alone except a few times when their grandmother didn't show up.

   ✧ Mrs. Lloyd has little money, but she heats the apartment and feeds and cares for her children the best she can with the little money she has.

   ✧ Mrs. Lloyd cares about her children and wants them to live with her.

   To prepare for the hearing, talk to Mrs. Lloyd. Make sure you understand the story she will tell at the hearing. Think about the questions you will ask her and the other witnesses. Ask the judge to explain the types of questions you are not allowed to ask, (see #3 Judge's part below).

3. **Judge** Your job is to listen to all the testimony. You may have to respond to requests made by the attorneys for your decision on certain questions and procedures. For example, lawyers may object to certain questions being asked or comments made by the lawyer or witness for the other side. Lawyers must follow certain rules, to insure fairness, in presenting evidence in court. Before the hearing, explain to the lawyers that they are not allowed to ask certain kinds of questions. In general, lawyers are *not* permitted to ask the following types of questions:

✧ Leading questions—Attorneys may not put words in the mouths of their *own* witnesses. For example, the juvenile court attorney who calls a social worker to **testify** should not ask questions calling for yes or no answers—"Isn't it true that you found cuts and bruises on Mrs. Smith's little boy?" This is a leading question. Instead, the attorney should ask a question like, "Would you describe the physical condition of Mrs. Smith's little boy when you examined him?" Leading questions are permitted on cross-examination.

✧ Opinion questions from unqualified witnesses—Witnesses are supposed to describe first-hand experiences. Questions should allow a witness to testify as to what he or she saw, heard, touched, tasted, smelled. Questions should not ask the witness to give an opinion unless the witness is qualified to give an opinion. For example, it would be improper for an attorney to ask a neighbor, who has no medical expertise, a question like, "In your opinion, is Mrs. Smith's little boy healthy?" The neighbor is not a qualified doctor, and cannot give an expert opinion to that question. On the other hand, a qualified person (like a medical doctor) may give an opinion if sufficient evidence has been given in court to qualify this witness as an expert in the field being discussed. What evidence might you present to qualify a doctor to answer a question like, "In your opinion, is Mrs. Smith's little boy healthy?"

✧ Badger or browbeat the witness—Attorneys must respect witnesses. Attorneys should not ask questions that attack a witness' reputation or pick on a witness. For example, it is improper for an opposing attorney to crowd a witness, point his or her finger, and repeatedly ask something like, "But isn't it true Mrs. Smith that you are a liar?"

If any of these types of questions are asked, the opposing attorney may make a request to the judge to throw out the question. For example, the attorney who believes a question is improper may say, "Objection your honor. The counsel (attorney) is badgering the witness." Based on the judge's interpretations of the question, the judge may *sustain* the objection (throw out the question) or *overrule* the objection (permit the question and require the witness to answer the question if possible).

After the lawyers have asked the witnesses questions, you may also question the witnesses or the lawyers if you don't understand something. It is your responsibility to decide if Robbie and Danny are being abused and/or neglected. Make your decision based on facts that are brought out at the hearing.

If you decide Robbie and Danny are abused and/or neglected, you must then decide what needs to be done about it. You will make this decision after you read and listen to the recommendation made by the social worker. The possible choices are described in the social worker's responsibility discussed on page 105.

4. **Court Reporter** It is your job to take down every word that is said by the lawyers, judge, and witnesses during the hearing. In actual hearings, court reporters have machines they use to take down every word quickly. The words you take down become a transcript. A transcript is a formal record of everything presented as "on the record" in a case. If someone has a question about the case later on, he or she would examine the transcript. Since you won't be able to use this machine, try to locate a tape recorder that you could use the day of the hearing. In some jurisdictions, tape recorders are also used for court reporting.

5. **Bailiff** Your job is to keep order in the courtroom. You take care of misconduct or an emergency; for example, if there is any unruly behavior or if someone faints or gets sick.

6. **Clerk** Your job is to swear in the witnesses when they come up to the witness stand. It is also your job to handle any evidence or documents.

7. **Guardian Ad Litem** You are the lawyer who represents only the child. In some courts there are trained guardian ad litems who are not attorneys. They may be volunteers who are trained to look after the best interests of the juvenile involved. During the hearing when the court decides what should be done with the child, it is your job to make sure that the action taken is in the best interests of the child. You can ask the lawyers or any witness questions during the adjudicatory and dispositional part of the hearing. Remember, a parent accused of neglect or abuse has the right to be represented by an attorney. The state, or juvenile court, is also represented by an attorney. Because of the possibility that the child's best interests might become lost, a guardian ad litem is appointed to represent the child independently.

Instructions to the Witness

It is your job to present the facts AS YOU SEE THEM. As a witness in a legal proceeding, you are sworn to answer all questions truthfully and to the best of your knowledge. If you do not know the answer to a question, simply tell the attorney or the judge "I don't know." If any question is unclear, ask the attorney or the judge to explain further. The following persons will be called to testify at the hearing. The testimony of each witness should be based on the background statements provided below. Remember, attorneys will be asking questions based on the background information.

8. **Robbie** You are the ten-year-old son of Mrs. Lloyd. This is your testimony: "I am ten years old. My brother, Danny, is two years old. I babysit him when my mom goes out. Sometimes she is gone when I get home from school and doesn't come home until after I go to bed. One day I stayed home

from school to take care of Danny. I can do things for my-self. I make my own breakfast every day. We don't have much food, and I get hungry a lot."

9. **Social Worker, Mr. Barry Horwitz** You work for the Division of Family Services. You have been a social worker for three years. You investigate reports of child abuse. During the hearing the juvenile court attorney will ask you to give a full report on the case of Robbie and Danny Lloyd. This is your testimony: "On January 6, I called on the Lloyds to investigate the report made by their neighbor. I found that they lived in a small apartment. Only space heaters were used to heat the apartment. These are dangerous around young children. There was hardly any food and no phone in the home. Mrs. Lloyd said she only left her boys alone at home when it was necessary. She tried to get their grand-mother to babysit, because she had no money to pay baby-sitters. On the first visit I warned her that it was danger-ous to leave a ten-year-old alone with a two-year-old be-cause the responsibility is too great. After the second Hot Line report in February, I called on Mrs. Lloyd again. I found nothing changed in the apartment. I noticed scars on Robbie's legs that looked like they were made with a strap or an extension cord. Mrs. Lloyd admitted she beat Robbie with a strap to punish him. Mrs. Lloyd told me to mind my own business and leave her alone."

10. **Mrs. Mary Lloyd** You are the mother of two children. You are accused of abusing and neglecting your children. This is your testimony: "I am twenty-six years old. I work odd hours doing cleaning mostly. The boys' grandmother says she will babysit when I need to go out, then she doesn't show up. What am I supposed to do? We are poor. I do the best I can. I think Robbie is old enough to make his own breakfast and to look after Danny sometimes. I sometimes whip Robbie when he misbehaves. I think that is the best way to make him mind."

11. **Mrs. Martha Cooper, Grandmother** You are Mrs. Lloyd's mother and the grandmother of Robbie and Danny. This is your testimony: "I can babysit, but I never know for sure when I'm supposed to. I can babysit at night but not during

the day because of my job. My daughter doesn't like me in her business, so I don't offer advice unless she asks me. There were a few times I didn't show up for babysitting because I got sick. And I couldn't call because they don't have a telephone."

·   ·   ·   · **Facts to Know**   ·   ·   ·   ·

Perhaps you have noticed that Danny Lloyd is not being called upon as a witness. Can you think of any reason why? In order to testify in court, a witness must be **competent** to do so. "Competence" generally means that the witness is mature and intelligent enough to understand the nature and purpose of the judicial proceeding. Witnesses must be able to understand their duty to tell the truth. Extremely young children, such as two-year-old Danny Lloyd, are usually not "competent" to be witnesses. The judge must sometimes decide if a young child is competent to be a witness by meeting with and questioning the child in the judge's chambers before being sworn in as a witness in formal court. As you can see, Robbie Lloyd was considered competent to be a witness.

·   ·   ·   ·   ·   ·   ·   ·   ·   ·   ·   ·   ·

—————————— A MOCK JUVENILE HEARING ——————————

I. THE ADJUDICATION

Bailiff:

Please remain seated. The court of Judge _____ will come to order.

Judge:

What do we have on the docket today?

Juvenile court attorney:

This is the matter of Robert and Daniel Lloyd. The people present in the courtroom are (*name all people present in courtroom who are involved in the case*). The children, Robert, age ten and Daniel, age two, are in the courtroom. Shall I read the charges made in the petition?

Defense attorney:

Yes.

Juvenile court attorney:

(*Reads the petition. Then says*) Do you admit or deny this petition?

Defense attorney:

I deny the petition.

Juvenile court attorney:

I call (*name of first witness, Barry Horwitz*) to the stand.

Judge:

Be sworn in by the clerk.

Clerk:

Hold up your right hand. Do you swear that the testimony you give in this case will be the whole truth and nothing but the truth?

The juvenile court attorney begins questioning his or her witnesses. Then the defense attorney can cross-examine these witnesses. After all the witnesses for the juvenile court attorney have testified, the defense attorney may call witnesses. The juvenile court attorney will have a chance to cross-examine the defense attorney's witnesses. The guardian ad litem also may question each witness. Each witness must be sworn in by the clerk before taking the stand.

· · · · **Facts to Know** · · · ·

admit—means agree with, accept as true
deny—means disagree with, declare untrue

If the defense lawyer admits the petition, there is no need to prove the facts of the case. The disposition would start then.

. . . .

Judge:

(After hearing the testimony given by the witnesses and asking them questions of your own, you must decide if Robbie and Danny have suffered child abuse and neglect. State your decision to the court.)

If the judge decides that this is a case of child abuse and/or neglect, the hearing will move directly into the second part—the DISPOSITION. If the judge decides that there is no child abuse and/or neglect, the hearing is over.

II. THE DISPOSITION (Usually Immediately Follows the Judge's Finding of Abuse and/or Neglect)

Juvenile court attorney:

"I want to call the social worker back to the stand. Have you made a careful study of the case of Robbie and Danny Lloyd? Are you ready to make a recommendation to the court?"

Social worker: (Before making your recommendation, read page 105.)

"Yes, I have studied the case carefully. In the past month I was able to help Mrs. Lloyd find a steady job as a waitress. She will work in the evenings when her mother can babysit with the boys. The grandmother has agreed to do this. Mrs. Lloyd will have more money now to care for her family. I am still concerned that her way of punishing her boys could be harmful to them. Also of concern is the fact that Mrs. Lloyd does not provide nutritious food. She needs to purchase a better, safer heater for the apartment. She says she wants the boys with her. I am recommending _____

_____ *(at this point explain your recommendations to the court)*."

The Dispositional Recommendation

Part of the social worker's responsibility at the dispositional hearing is to present a recommendation to the judge about what might be done to help the Lloyd family. The social worker must also explain to the judge why he believes that his recommendation is the best one available. Typical recommendations are that the court:

✧ Order counseling for one or more family members.

✧ Order classes in parenting and child care.

✧ Allow a child to stay with the family under supervision of a social worker.

✧ Place a child in a foster home for a short time.

✧ Place a child in a foster home for a long time.

✧ Commit child or family member to be evaluated by doctors.

✧ Terminate (end completely) parental rights and have child adopted by another family.

The social worker witness should prepare such a recommendation to present to the judge at the dispositional hearing. The report should be in writing and should set forth the recommendation and the reasons supporting it.

Guardian ad litem:

(Questions the social worker and anyone else involved in the hearing to make sure that the recommendations are in the best interest of the boys.)
At this point, each of the lawyers and the judge may ask questions of anyone involved in the hearing. The mother, the grandmother, and Robbie can be questioned to make sure they are willing to follow through on their responsibilities.

Judge:

(At the end of the discussion, the judge states the disposition.)

"It is therefore ordered that the juveniles be_____."

Debriefing: What Did You Learn?

1. Do you think the hearing was a fair way to resolve (work out) this problem of possible child abuse and neglect? Did you feel the judge's decision was fair to the children and to the parent? Explain your reasons.

2. Were all the facts necessary to decide the case brought out at the hearing? Briefly describe some of the most important facts and identify any that you think were left out. Why do you think these facts were important to the case?

3. If you had been the neighbor would you have called the child abuse Hot Line Service? Explain why or why not.

4. If you had been the social worker, what recommendations would you have made to the judge? Explain why you would make these recommendations.

5. If you were the judge in this case, what do you think about the way Mrs. Lloyd handled her boys? For example, do you think it was all right for her to leave Robbie and Danny at home alone? What would you have decided if you had been the judge?

6. What kind of help do you think it is most important for the Lloyd family to get?

7. What were some important things you learned from putting on your own mock juvenile hearing?

8. What do you think needs to be done to help prevent child abuse and neglect?

Activity #1

Put on your mock hearing for another class, school or a parent meeting. At the end of the hearing discuss the debriefing questions on page 106. If possible, have someone from the court, a judge, a lawyer or a guardian ad litem, discuss the questions with your group and also discuss the hearing procedure.

Activity #2

Put together information about the different services in your community that help prevent child abuse and neglect. The information could be distributed in your community through a report or pamphlet. In your findings you might discover additional services that are needed and they could be described in your report.

Activity #3

Find out if your juvenile court has a volunteer guardian ad litem program. If one exists you could contact the organization and find out ways that you could help. For example, you might help them publicize their work, or help recruit volunteers to be trained as guardian ad litems.

· EXTRA ·

Find out about how your local or state child abuse and neglect hotline works including such information as what happens after a report is made and what kind of follow up occurs. You can probably get some information from the library or by contacting a government agency dealing with youth and families, like The Division of Family Services.

✧ ✧ Vocabulary Words ✧ ✧

bailiff
child abuse
child welfare
clear and convincing evidence
clerk
competent
court reporter

evidence
foster care
guardian ad litem
neglect
parens patriae
testify

LESSON 12

Theory and Practice in the Juvenile Court

Objectives

As a result of this lesson, students will be able to:

✧ Recognize and explain the difference between theory and practice in certain aspects of the juvenile court.

✧ Explain what it means to be a status offender.

✧ Analyze and explain how juvenile court judges are influenced by a number of different facts and issues.

✧ Recognize and explain that a juvenile court judge has responsibility to the individual offender as well as to society.

In the last few lessons you have learned a number of things about how the law affects you as a juvenile, the reasons behind the establishment of a separate court for juveniles, and the legal process involved when juveniles enter the juvenile court system.

This system of laws and procedures for juveniles was developed to serve their special needs for care and protection as well as for discipline and punishment. The theory behind these special laws and procedures says that:

⟡ The juvenile court CAN protect a juvenile from harm, abuse, and neglect.

⟡ The juvenile court CAN help a juvenile change his or her ways.

⟡ The juvenile court CAN punish juveniles who break the law and it IS the appropriate agency for doing so.

⟡ The juvenile court CAN protect society from juveniles who break the law and it IS the appropriate agency for doing so.

However, there are often gaps between the way things are supposed to be and the way things are. As with many things, in juvenile court some things are often different in **theory** (how it is supposed to be) than in **practice** (how it really happens).

What should be done to make sure the theory becomes part of the practice? Read on and continue to think about this question.

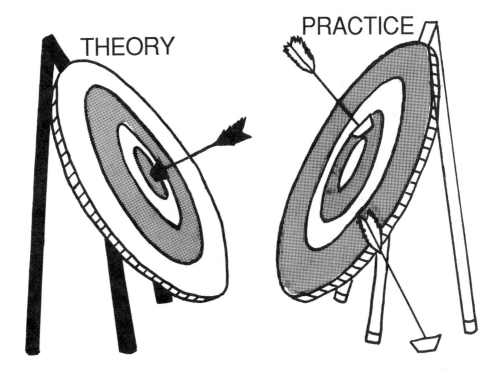

THEORY AND PRACTICE AND THE STATUS OFFENDER

A **status offense** is an act which is illegal only if committed by a juvenile. For example, it is illegal for a 14-year-old to run away from home but it is not illegal for a 24-year-old to run away from home.

Examples of status offenses are running away from home, and being truant from school. What are some other status offenses? There is a gap between theory and practice in handling status offenders.

THEORY

PRACTICE

Theory Says:

The juvenile court has a right to take control of a juvenile if he or she is in need of supervision, but has not committed a "crime."

Practice Shows:

Juveniles who are status offenders enter the juvenile court system and, in some instances, may be placed with young people who have committed more serious crimes. By being placed with serious offenders, the status offenders may begin to see themselves as lawbreakers rather than as people needing help.

What do you think about the juvenile theory of status offenses? Explain your answers. Below you will have a chance to analyze the theory and practice of status offenses as it relates to juveniles.

YOU BE THE JUDGE

Pretend you are the juvenile court judge who has to decide the following cases. You can choose the decision you think is best from the list following each case. You must give reasons to support the decisions you make. Remember, every judge has a responsibility to protect the community. This responsibility must be weighed against the desire to help a young person.

James

James is 13. He has not attended school regularly for six months. By law James is required to attend school until he is 16. According to the juvenile code of his state, James was found to be truant from school and was taken into custody by the juvenile court. James' parents both work. They are unable to make sure James goes to and stays at school every day. James says school is worthless. He likes spending time with older friends who don't go to school either. Some of these friends have been arrested and some convicted for drug-related crimes. Some are awaiting trial on criminal charges.

Points to Discuss Before Making a Decision

In what ways might it hurt society if young people don't go to school? In what ways might it hurt James to be truant from school? As judge you could:

1. Order James home with his parents and issue a warning to James and his parents reminding them that James must attend school.

2. Place James on probation with the requirement he must go to school and report to his juvenile officer once a week. His probation can last from two months to one year.

3. Send James away from home for one year to a training school.

4. Place James in a state institution for boys for six months.

5. Make the parents pay a fine if James does not go to school.

6. Your own idea.

What is your decision? Give a good reason why you decided the way you did.

Carla

Carla was taken into custody by the juvenile court for being a runaway. This is the second time she has come to juvenile court for running away, although she has admitted to running away several times. The first time was one year ago. At that time she was placed on probation and had to report to a juvenile officer once a week for six months. Carla is 15 years old. Carla's mother and father say they can't control Carla anymore. Carla says she is unhappy and bored at home. She has stayed with other runaways, and she has gotten into serious trouble during these previous trips. Each time, she has stayed away from home about three weeks and then returned.

Points to Discuss Before Making a Decision

In what way might young runaways harm a society? In what ways might young runaways be hurting themselves? As judge you could:

1. Let Carla return home in her parents' custody.

2. Place Carla on probation with the requirement she must stay at home and not run away, and report to a juvenile officer once a week for six months.

3. Send Carla away to a training program for a few months.

4. Place Carla in a state institution for girls for six months.

5. Your own idea.

What is your decision? Give a good reason for deciding the way you did.

"Young people come into court as status offenders because they have problems. Their problems often affect the community. The juvenile court seems to be the best agency to take custody of these young people. Greater efforts could be made to keep these juveniles separate from those who have committed crimes."

"I disagree. Young people who are status offenders should never come to juvenile court. They are not really criminals but people in need of help. There should be other places these young people can get help."

Who do **YOU** think should take responsibility for young people like James and Carla, who are status offenders?

Choose your answer from the list below:

✧ Their parents or guardian.

✧ Other young people who have been trained as youth counselors.

✧ The juvenile court system which includes places like training schools and foster homes.

✧ Help centers run by religious or social service agencies with adult counselors.

✧ No one. Let the young people take care of themselves.

✧ Specially trained people within a school system.

✧ Your additional ideas:_____

_____.

THEORY AND PRACTICE AND JUVENILE COURT JUDGES

There is also a gap between the way theory says that juvenile court judges should deal with young people who enter the court system and the way it really happens.

Theory Says:

✧ The judge acts somewhat like a parent.

✧ The judge makes a careful study of the facts and decides what treatment will best help the juvenile and also protect society.

✧ Juvenile judges should have expert knowledge of law and child psychology.

✧ They should know about effective treatment programs for youth and be able to send young people to the program that will help them most.

Practice Shows:

✧ Some judges treat juveniles almost the same as adult offenders.

✧ Some judges don't have adequate experience in juvenile court philosophy and procedures.

✧ Some have no special training in child psychology.

✧ Because of heavy case loads and limited number of juvenile courts, judges may not have time to research the available treatment programs carefully. In addition, effective training programs or group homes may be overcrowded or unavailable.

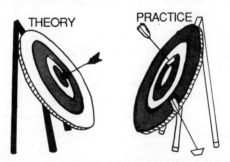

On the next page you will have a chance to analyze juvenile court theory and practice with a specific case example.

At an adjudicatory hearing, Frank Jones was found to have committed a purse snatching. Frank is thirteen years old. Frank's teachers say that he does pretty well in school, although he sometimes gets in trouble for taking things that do not belong to him. Frank's father works long hours. Frank's mother is home, and she spends a lot of time with Frank when he's home. This is Frank's first offense in juvenile court. Frank must now face a dispositional hearing where a judge must recommend what should be done with him. Read the paragraphs about Judge Lopez, Judge Ackman, and Judge Pham below and decide which of the following four alternatives each one might choose.

1. Let Frank go with a warning.

2. Put Frank on probation in the care of his mother and father for six months. He would have to report to his juvenile officer once a week.

3. Send Frank to a group home.

4. Send Frank to a state institution for boys.

Judge Miranda Lopez

"My name is Judge Miranda Lopez. I have five children of my own, and I believe in punishing them if they misbehave. I do like children very much and believe they should be treated fairly. Some people say I should be a stricter judge and others say that I am too strict. I want to protect both the rights of the individual young person and the rights of society to be protected from crime. It is a difficult job. What alternative will I choose for Frank? Why?"

Judge Samuel Ackman

"My name is Judge Samuel Ackman. I just came to the juvenile court from the family and divorce courts. The city and the state do not have adequate centers to treat juveniles so that delinquent juveniles can get help. Because there are no places to send juveniles, I try to put them back in their homes and give them adequate care with a counselor. What alternative will I choose for Frank? Why?"

Judge Chanti Pham

"My name is Judge Chanti Pham. I have been a judge for 12 years. I live in the city with my wife and two sons. In the last four years, juvenile crime in my city has doubled, and the city is blaming me. I won't stand for any more juveniles committing crimes. If I punish Frank severely, perhaps it will influence other juveniles not to commit crimes. My wife had her purse stolen last year. I am responsible for protecting society. What alternative will I choose for Frank? Why?"

Questions for Discussion

---

1. Imagine you were the juvenile judge for Frank Jones' dispositional hearing. What alternative would you choose for Frank? Why?

2. If Frank were sent to a state institution for boys, what do you think he would be like when he came out? Do you think he would ever steal a purse again? Would he commit other offenses? What reasons do you have for your answer?

3. When Judge Lopez said that she "wanted to protect both the rights of the individual and the rights of society" what do you think she meant?

4. Judges are often limited in their decisions about what to do with juveniles because the available alternatives are not as effective as they could be. Discuss the following "what if" situations. How would this additional information influence your recommendations for Frank Jones?

What If . . .

you as judge knew the probation officer had many more cases than he or she could effectively handle?

What If . . .

you knew the state juvenile institution was overcrowded?

What If . . .

you knew the group home that accepted Frank also had some juveniles who had committed very serious crimes?

What If . . .

Frank's mother was unable to take care of him or supervise him very well?

Could these "what if " situations make a difference in your decision about what to do with Frank? Why or why not?

As a class, you could conduct a short survey of juvenile court judges in your city or state. For each judge that you contact, describe Frank's case and ask them which of the four alternatives on page 115 they would choose and why, or ask the judge to offer another alternative that he or she might recommend. Select one or more students to be responsible for each of the following tasks:

1. Finding the names and addresses of juvenile court judges.

2. Developing a survey form.

3. Writing a cover letter describing the class project and what you are asking the judges to do.

4. Serving as reviewers and editors of the survey form and letter.

5. Analyzing the survey results.

6. Writing a report on the results.

7. Sharing the report with other classes in your school.

8. Writing a thank-you letter to the judges who participate.

· E X T R A ·

In 1974 Congress passed the Juvenile Justice and Delinquency Prevention Act. One important goal of this Act is to find alternatives for juveniles in trouble other than locking them up. Using the newspaper, find articles about juveniles who have been taken into custody by the police or juvenile authorities. For each article answer the following:

✧ Why was the juvenile taken into custody?

✧ Where is the juvenile being held?

✧ According to the article, what might happen to the juvenile?

✧ Based on the information you have read, what do you think should be done with this juvenile? Be able to explain your answer.

✧ ✧ **Vocabulary Words** ✧ ✧

practice   **theory**
status offense

LESSON 13

Juvenile Crime and Consequences

Objectives

As a result of this lesson, students will be able to:

✧ Identify crimes often committed by juveniles.

✧ Describe the role of the legislative branch of government in identifying and classifying crimes and their punishments.

✧ Analyze crimes often committed by juveniles and evaluate the seriousness of these actions and their legal consequences.

S tudy the illustrations on the next two pages. Each illustration represents situations involving juveniles. After you have studied the pictures, answer the following questions:

1. What is happening in each picture? What, if any, offense is occurring?

2. Is anyone being harmed by what is happening in the picture? Briefly describe who, if anyone, is being harmed, and explain how they are harmed by the offense.

The actions shown in these pictures are all serious crimes. A crime is an act forbidden by law. A crime may also occur when someone fails to do something that the law requires. For example, a parent or legal guardian should provide basic necessities such as food, shelter, clothing, and health care for a minor child. If the parent or legal guardian fails to provide these necessities, the guardian may be charged with endangering the welfare of a child.

Crimes affect juveniles as well as adults. Juveniles commit crimes and they are also victims of crimes. According to recent studies by the U.S. Department of Justice, juveniles are more likely to be victims of crime than any other age group.

Juveniles are often treated according to the seriousness of their offense. For example, a thirteen-year-old who commits a crime such as **armed robbery** is likely to receive a much different disposition than a thirteen-year-old who commits an act of **vandalism**.

THE LEGISLATIVE BRANCH: Criminal Codes

The legislative branch of government has the responsibility for defining crimes and establishing a range of punishments. Most laws and definitions of crime are passed by the state legislature, although some are passed by Congress and local lawmakers. Crimes are classified into three categories:

Ordinance Violations

Ordinances are laws passed by local or county lawmaking bodies. Examples of ordinances are laws governing curfew, traffic, speed limits, safety, and sanitation in the community including anti-littering ordinances. Persons violating ordinances are usually punished by paying fines, although some offenders may be punished by a short period in jail.

Misdemeanors

These offenses are often referred to as less serious, or minor, offenses. **Misdemeanors** are punishable by less than a year in a local or county jail, as well as by fine. Examples of misdemeanors are **driving while intoxicated** or under the influence, vandalism, **petty theft**, and **simple assault**.

Felonies

A **felony** usually refers to a more serious, or major, crime. These crimes are punishable by a year or more in a state prison, and sometimes include a fine as well. Examples of felonies are **murder, vehicular homicide,** armed robbery, **aggravated assault, rape, arson, fraud,** and **embezzlement.**

Review the illustrations on pages 120-121. Imagine you are a member of your state's legislature, and you are having to review your state's **criminal code** by deciding what actions are crimes. Answer the following about each picture.

1. Briefly describe the type of crime in the picture. For example, if a picture shows someone intentionally setting fire to someone else's property, the type of crime would be "arson."

2. Identify why each action should be considered a crime.

3. Classify the actions you have listed as crimes into the following categories: (You may wish to prepare a chart like the one on page 124 for further clarification.)

  ✧ "felony" actions;

  ✧ "misdemeanor" actions;

  ✧ "ordinance violations."—If you believe this is an ordinance violation then you should be able to explain why this crime is better for local lawmakers to handle than your state legislature.

4. Rank the actions from most serious crimes to least serious crimes.

	Is this a felony?	Is this a misdemeanor?	Is this an ordinance violation?	Rank from most serious (1) to least serious (11)
A.	?	?	?	?
B.	?	?	?	?
C.	?	?	?	?
D.	'?	?	?	?
E.	?	?	?	?
F.	?	?	?	?
G.	?	?	?	?
H.	?	?	?	?
I.	?	?	?	?
J.	?	?	?	?
K.	?	?	?	?

5. Are there other crimes, not pictured, that you believe affect juveniles? If yes, describe those crimes and explain their legal consequences.

6. In your opinion, should any of these situations not be classified as crimes? Briefly explain your answer.

MAKING A DIFFERENCE

Survey your family and friends by having them do the ranking activity on pages 123-124. Compare and contrast their responses with those of students in your class. You may wish to write an article for your school or local newspaper regarding your survey results.

· ─── E X T R A ─── ·

Using the library, research your state laws regarding felonies and misdemeanors. How are these crimes defined in your state? Select several examples of felonies and misdemeanors. Describe the penalties for committing these crimes established by your legislature.

aggravated assault
armed robbery
arson
criminal code
driving while intoxicated
embezzlement
felony
fraud

misdemeanor
murder
ordinance
petty theft
rape
simple assault
vandalism
vehicular homicide

LESSON 14

Consequences of Action to the Juvenile Offender

Objectives

As a result of this lesson, students will be able to:

✧ Recognize and analyze possible consequences of crime for the offender.

✧ Identify and analyze factors influencing decisions to certify juveniles as adults.

✧ Apply and evaluate factors influencing decisions to certify juveniles as adults in specific transfer hearing cases.

In Lesson 1, consequences of action were discussed, and throughout the book you have studied the consequences of the actions of others. Do you believe that most people think about the consequences of their actions? Why? Why not?

The situations on the next pages describe actions taken by juveniles. Imagine that you are a reporter. You are assigned to write a newspaper headline and short news story to go with each of the following situations. Your news story should describe consequences for the person or persons in each situation. The example below will help you to get started.

EXAMPLE

Two boys were walking late at night. One boy said to the other, "This parking lot is closed at night. Let's climb over the fence and see what's inside."

Possible Headline:

YOUNG BOY CLIMBING FENCE IS MAULED BY DOG

Possible Story:

Two thirteen-year-old boys climbed over a fence at Acme Parking Lot, 4130 Grace. One of the boys was badly hurt when a watchdog attacked him. The other boy said that they did not see the dog approaching. "The dog seemed to come from out of nowhere," he said. The hospitalized boy is in serious condition.

Develop headlines and stories for the following situations:

1. A group of young people were drinking beer and wine at Russell's house. They decided to take Russell's mother's car. "My mother doesn't care," said Russell. "Nothing will happen."

Possible Headline . . .

Possible Story . . .

2. "I'm running away," thought fourteen-year-old Alicia. "I'll hitchhike to my friend's place in California."

Possible Headline . . .

Possible Story . . .

3. "I'll look out for you," eighteen-year-old Brad told thirteen-year-old Allen, handing Allen a switch-blade knife. Brad said, "You're still a juvenile. Just hold the knife on the old man while I take his wallet."

Possible Headline . . .

Possible Story . . .

4. "My friends gave me this good 'stuff' and said it would make me feel really good. One time won't hurt."

Possible Headline . . .

Possible Story . . .

5. "The old lady will let go of her purse when you grab it. Just do it and don't worry," eighteen-year-old Ed said to fifteen-year-old Manuel.

Possible Headline . . .

Possible Story . . .

THINK about your headlines and stories. Which ones had the most serious consequences? Which ones had the least serious consequences? Explain why. Review the stories. Describe what laws might be involved with each story.

WHEN JUVENILES ARE TREATED AS ADULTS

LaWanda, 14, is caught after running away from home. Larry, 13, is picked up for being out past curfew. Terry, 15, is taken into custody for **kidnapping,** robbing, and shooting a 21-year-old.

Who's going to take custody of LaWanda, Larry, and Terry, and what's going to happen to them? What do you think should happen to them?

Each of these juvenile **offenders** will initially be taken into juvenile custody. In most juvenile jurisdictions, a juvenile officer will review the circumstances and file a petition outlining the nature of the offense.

What offenses do you think these three teens committed?

LaWanda and Larry would be charged with status offenses—offenses that only affect juveniles. Terry's charges are considered legally more serious; and if he were older (in most jurisdictions 17 or 18), he would automatically be tried as an adult on felony charges. Some people believe that the maturity of a 15-year-old is not that much different from that of a 17-year-old. They believe that most fifteen-year-olds know right from wrong. To them, Terry should know that kidnapping, **robbery,** and aggravated assault are wrong. Terry should face the consequences of his actions, just like an adult. In your opinion, should most juveniles who commit serious offenses be treated as adults? Explain your answer.

You have probably seen or heard news stories about teenagers being tried for murder and even sentenced to prison. When can juveniles be treated and tried as adults? Every state has a special procedure for deciding the question of when to transfer juveniles to adult criminal jurisdiction. This decision and process of certifying juveniles as adults is determined by state law. The law must follow state and federal constitutional guidelines. The Constitution is interpreted by decisions of the U.S. Supreme Court. In the case *Kent v. United States* (1966), the U.S. Supreme Court ordered that all juveniles have a right to a **due process hearing**. The due process guidelines provide for a juvenile to have many of the same fifth and fourteenth amendment rights as an adult (for example, the right to an attorney and the right to examine all evidence in the case).

In most cases, a juvenile court judge holds a **certification or transfer hearing** to decide if a young person should be tried as an adult. In reaching this decision, the judge hears evidence and considers many of the same factors discussed in Lesson 11 including the following suggested by the U.S. Supreme Court in the Kent case:

1. The seriousness of the offense (for example, was the act committed in a violent or willful manner, and did it result in damage to property or injury to persons?).

2. The amount of evidence supporting the **allegation** (that is, is there strong evidence to indicate that the juvenile did commit the offense?).

3. Adult involvement (for example, is there an adult who is an **accomplice** in the offense? Should the juvenile be treated the same as the adult who is involved?).

4. The maturity of the juvenile (for example, what is the juvenile's age, does the juvenile appear and act as an adult in most situations? Does the juvenile understand the difference between right and wrong?).

5. Previous juvenile record (for example, has the juvenile been in trouble with the law on previous occasions? How often has the juvenile been in juvenile court? What has the court decided in the past offenses and has the juvenile obeyed the court's decisions?).

6. The likelihood of **rehabilitation** if treated as a juvenile offender (for example, if kept in juvenile jurisdiction, will the juvenile correct his or her behavior? Does the juvenile have family support? Does the juvenile have a good school record?).

Read each of the following cases. Imagine you are a juvenile judge hearing these cases. Read each case and decide if the juvenile(s) should be certified as an adult. Briefly explain your answer.

CASE 1

While recklessly driving without a license, Jerry, 16, hits a school bus head-on. The bus bursts into flames. Twenty-seven young people die in the crash, and thirty-three are seriously injured. Jerry and an eighteen-year-old friend, Keith, survive the crash with minor injuries. Evidence indicates that Keith and Jerry were probably drinking. Jerry's blood alcohol content at the time of the accident makes him legally intoxicated. As a result of a previous incident, Jerry has had his license suspended for driving while intoxicated. Keith, an adult, also has one **DWI** conviction.

Jerry is an above-average student in school. He lives with both of his parents. Jerry's father is an alcoholic and has on occasion beaten Jerry. Jerry likes school but hates his home life. Other than the previous DWI conviction, Jerry has never been in trouble with the law. Jerry also claims Keith pressured him into getting drunk.

Should Jerry be certified to stand trial as an adult on the charges of **vehicular manslaughter** (murder with an automobile while in an intoxicated condition) and **vehicular injury** (aggravated assault with an automobile while in an intoxicated condition)? Why or why not?

CASE 2

Jane, 15, runs away with her boyfriend, Jack, 16. They travel to a neighboring state. Jane and Jack have a hard time making a living, and Jane has just had a baby. They both dropped out of high school. Jack finds work for minimum wage at a fast food restaurant. Jane has to stay home with their baby. Jack suggests that they should think about giving up the baby because

they are not able to afford taking care of her. After a long discussion, Jack and Jane decide to leave the child, wrapped in a blanket, on the steps of a church. Feeling depressed about abandoning their child, Jane and Jack start drinking heavily and both eventually become drunk and pass out. During the night, the baby becomes cold and ill. When someone at the church finds the baby, the baby is rushed to the emergency room at a nearby hospital. The baby is diagnosed as having pneumonia and dies.

Soon after, the police take Jane and Jack into custody. Jack and Jane admit to abandoning the baby but claim they meant no harm. They were trying to leave the baby in a decent place. Jane has a juvenile record of running away. Jack has no juvenile record. Jack's mother and father offer to take Jane and Jack into their home until they get back on their feet.

Should Jane and Jack be certified to stand trial as adults charged with **manslaughter, endangering the welfare of a child,** and **abandoning a child**?

Why or why not?

CASE 3

Jim, age 14, and a group of guys he hangs out with, had been drinking some beer and wine, and some had been smoking marijuana. Some of the guys are 18. Jim is the youngest in the group although he acts older than his age.

Jim and the group break into Central High one night. They vandalize the media center, causing hundreds of dollars in damages. They take some of the computers and one of the VCRs out of the school. One of the guys tells Jim that they can use the computers to break into the school's computer records and really mess up students' grades and records.

A janitor sees the guys carrying the computers and begins to chase them. Jim is almost caught by the janitor, but just before the janitor reaches Jim, the janitor slips and falls on the pavement. The guys manage to get away with some of the computers and a VCR. The janitor is able to get to a telephone and call the police. The janitor is taken to a hospital and is treated for some bruises and a broken wrist. The janitor identifies Jim because the janitor remembers how nice Jim is in school.

Jim is taken into custody by the police. Jim lives with his mother and four other brothers and sisters. Jim's mother and father are divorced. His mother works two jobs in order to raise all of the children. Jim has been in juvenile jurisdiction for illegal possession of alcohol twice before.

Should Jim be tried as an adult for **breaking and entering**? For vandalism? For aggravated assault? For computer-related crimes? Why or why not?

The issue of certification of juveniles is very important as more and more states are debating changes in the law to allow for more juveniles to be treated legally as adults in certain types of cases.

Working with your teacher and principal, your class could plan a panel discussion to address the issue of juvenile certification. You may want to invite a juvenile judge or hearing officer, an attorney who handles juvenile cases, and a legislator to be on your panel. Before the panel meets, develop some questions you want to ask each panelist and share them with all panel members. You might invite other classes to hear the discussion, or it could be held at an open community meeting sponsored by your class, your school's parent organization, and neighborhood organizations.

--- EXTRA ---

What guidelines does your state use in determining the transfer of juveniles to adult courts? (At what age may juveniles be transferred, who makes the transfer decision, and what factors influence the decision?) Answers to these questions may be found in your state statutes (under juvenile code) in the library, or you may wish to contact the juvenile court.

✧ ✧ Vocabulary Words ✧ ✧

abandoning a child
accomplice
allegation
breaking and entering
certification or transfer
   hearing
due process hearing
DWI (driving while intoxicated)
endangering the welfare
   of a child

kidnapping
manslaughter
offenders
rehabilitation
robbery
vehicular injury
vehicular manslaughter

LESSON 15

Judging Juveniles: Rehabilitation or Punishment

Objectives

As a result of this lesson, students will be able to:

❖ Define and explain the terms "rehabilitation" and "punishment."

❖ Compare and contrast various points of view concerning rehabilitation and punishment for juvenile offenders.

Juveniles who find themselves in trouble with the law often appear caught in the middle—too young to be treated as an adult, too old not to be held responsible for their actions. So what should be done with them? People's opinions differ in answering this question.

These people are for stricter punishments for juveniles who commit crimes. What arguments might they be making for stricter punishments?

These people are for helping young people change to a way of life that is more acceptable to society. They want to make sure young people get help. What arguments might they be making for their position?

Some answers are:

✧ Soft or special treatment encourages juveniles to continue to commit crime.

✧ Juveniles are as dangerous to their victims as adults. They should be given tough punishments.

✧ If juveniles knew they would be locked up in jail, they would not commit as much crime.

✧ Set specific punishments for each offense.

Other answers are:

✧ Locking up kids doesn't solve their problems but adds more problems.

✧ Juveniles are young; they can change if they get help and guidance.

✧ Different kinds of programs need to be provided for juveniles which include rehabilitation.

✧ Treat each juvenile as an individual and don't set specific sentences for all juveniles.

Look at the definition of the word "REHABILITATION" and the picture of the word below. Does the picture describe the definition? Why or why not?

Word Definition:

Rehabilitation emphasizes restoring a person to a way of life which is useful and acceptable to society.

Picture Definition:

Name some activities or programs a young person might take part in that could help in his or her rehabilitation.

Why do you think these programs or activities could be helpful to a young person? Explain your answers.

Now look at the definition and a picture of the word **"PUNISHMENT"** on the following page. Does the picture describe the definition? Why or why not?

Can you provide an alternative definition of the word "punishment"? Explain whether you think punishment is a **deterrent** for a juvenile who might be considering committing an offense.

Word Definition:

Punishment emphasizes protection of society by taking offenders off the streets. It also emphasizes deterrence—making the consequences (being locked up in a state institution) severe enough to be an example to others not to commit crimes.

Picture Definition:

Describe this picture. Is this picture a realistic way to describe punishment? Explain your answer. What kind of punishment, if any, would you consider to be a deterrent? Why?

The questionnaire below is intended to help people better understand what their opinions are about rehabilitation and punishment for juvenile offenders. For each statement, choose the response which best represents your opinion and why.

Strongly agree
Agree
No opinion
Disagree
Strongly disagree

1. "Taxpayers should spend money for better rehabilitation places for juveniles in our community."

2. "The only way to handle juvenile crime is to put kids in a jail-like place that will make them regret ever getting into trouble."

3. "The way to rehabilitate is to give kids an experience in a place where they know people care about them and where they have to meet certain responsibilities."

4. "If they spent more money making the schools better, they wouldn't need to spend the money on rehabilitation centers because fewer young people would get into trouble."

5. "Kids don't need to be rehabilitated, they just need to know they can't get away with committing crimes without being punished."

6. "If juveniles were given stiffer punishment, there would not be as much juvenile crime."

7. "It depends on the person. All juvenile offenders are different. Some should be worked with and helped, and some should just be locked up."

8. "To rehabilitate people to become useful members of society, you have to make certain they feel good about themselves, feel they have some worth as human beings."

9. "Juveniles who commit crimes should be given jail sentences, not special help programs."

Consider the following case:

YOU decide what should happen to Karen.

Karen, a fifteen-year-old ninth-grade student, is arrested at school by an undercover police officer. She has marijuana in her purse and an index card with names of people who owe her money. She is charged with possession of marijuana with intent to distribute. Karen admits that she had been using marijuana and that she sometimes sells it. This is Karen's first serious offense in juvenile court.

1. In your opinion, should Karen be given rehabilitation or punishment? Explain your answer.

2. Look back over the statements on pages 137 and 140. Which statements fit the decision that you made? Why?

3. What might be appropriate rehabilitation for Karen? What might be appropriate punishment for Karen? Be able to explain reasons for your answers.

4. If you were a parent of a student Karen had sold marijuana to, what might you recommend—rehabilitation or punishment for Karen? Explain the parents' point of view.

You might want to give a copy of the questionnaire on page 140 to several people you know and ask them to complete it. Then bring back your findings and compare and contrast your survey results with other students in your class. Make a chart in class showing how people responded to these questions. Compare your survey results with other public opinion surveys, or polls, on rehabilitation and punishment. Your local librarian can help you find information on this topic. Share your analysis of the survey results by writing an article for the school or local newspaper.

· E X T R A ·

Throughout this text, you have had an opportunity to express your opinions about juvenile responsibility and law. Begin or add to your journal, "My Thoughts on the Treatment of Juveniles," and write your thoughts on how juveniles should be treated. You may wish to make comments on the opinions expressed by other students, or comments based on news stories or actual discussions with juvenile judges, attorneys, law enforcement officers, friends, and family members. Review your journal from time to time to see if your opinions have changed. If they have changed, explain your reasons.

✧ ✧ Vocabulary Words ✧ ✧

deterrent   punishment

LESSON 16

Dispositional Alternatives for Juveniles

Objectives

As a result of this lesson, students will be able to:

✧ Describe and analyze dispositional alternatives that may be ordered by juvenile court authorities.

✧ Analyze dispositional alternatives for juveniles in specific cases.

✧ Analyze whether there should be set penalties for juveniles.

In most cases, a juvenile judge is in charge of the adjudicatory hearing to decide the facts in cases involving young people who come before his or her court. In a few states, juries decide some types of juvenile cases. Using the **precedent** of the U.S. Supreme Court's decision, *In Re Winship* (1970), a judge and/or jury must find the juvenile guilty beyond a reasonable doubt, if the juvenile is charged with a serious offense. If a juvenile is found delinquent, the juvenile court will hold a dispositional hearing and decide to order one of several dispositional alternatives for the juvenile based on the specific needs of the juvenile and community. The following two pages explain the most commonly used dispositional alternatives.

DISPOSITIONAL ALTERNATIVES

A WARNING

Juveniles are not given a sentence but are warned that if they come to court again, the court will take a more severe action. They are then released to the care of a custodial parent or guardian.

OR

PROBATION COUNSELING

With probation, juveniles stay in their own homes and continue their usual activities. A deputy juvenile officer or juvenile counselor sees them regularly. During these counseling periods, the counselor can determine if they are fulfilling their responsibilities to school, work, and family.

OR

MANDATORY EDUCATION OR SPECIAL TREATMENT PROGRAM

Juveniles attend a special kind of **mandatory** education or treatment program as ordered by the juvenile court.

OR

GROUP HOME

A group home is a large house usually in the juvenile's own community. About ten or twelve young people live in the house with counselors who live and work there. The juveniles are responsible for going to school and/or work. The resident counselors check to make certain the juveniles are meeting these responsibilities. Each juvenile takes part in household activities, like cleaning and other chores.

OR

RESTITUTION

With **restitution,** the juveniles are ordered to pay back the **victims** in some way for the harm caused the victims.

OR

FOSTER CARE

Juveniles who have very serious problems at home can be placed in another home. Families agree to take in young people and make them part of their family. Counseling with the juvenile takes place regularly by a counselor assigned by the juvenile court.

OR

MINIMUM SECURITY CENTER

A minimum security center is usually a smaller place where juveniles are not locked in but where they must stay. These centers may even be farms where juveniles stay, work, and try to learn to live together in a positive way. Emphasis here is on educational activities and training programs. Juveniles are kept under close watch; most of their daily activities are scheduled for them.

OR

MAXIMUM SECURITY CENTER

This is often a large state institution housing several hundred boys or girls. Many states have one place for boys and one for girls. Usually they are outside major city areas. Juveniles are kept under close watch, and their daily activities are entirely set for them. Young people are locked in and cannot leave. Activities in these institutions vary, but juveniles are required to attend some kind of school while they are there.

OR

CERTIFICATION AS AN ADULT

Juveniles may be certified as adults under certain conditions. As adults, their cases are tried in adult criminal court, and they may receive an adult penalty. Juveniles can be certified as adults for serious crimes such as armed robbery, murder, rape, or if they have a long record of serious violations.

Use the dispositional alternatives on the previous pages in deciding what should happen to the juveniles in the following cases. Explain your decisions. For example, if you decide to place a juvenile in a home or institution, how long would he or she have to stay, and why? If you decide to make the juvenile pay back the victim, in what way would payment be made?

In making your decisions, remember that it is the juvenile judge's duty to help a young person change for the better, as well as to protect society from being harmed by juvenile lawbreakers. In each of these cases, the judge found the juveniles delinquent—guilty as charged. You must decide what disposition will be made in each case.

STORY 1

Jeff said to Danny, "Old man Daws didn't have any right to kick us out of his pet store and call us bums. Let's get his store tonight. We'll show him he can't get away with treating us like dirt." These boys were caught by the police throwing bricks into Mr. Daws' window. One brick broke the glass on a large tank of exotic and rare tropical fish. The rare and valuable fish all died. The bricks destroyed several thousand dollars in merchandise, including the tank of expensive tropical fish. The police took the boys (ages 14 and 15) to the juvenile court.

At a later adjudicatory hearing, the juvenile judge ruled that Jeff and Danny had committed the act of vandalism and destruction of property—felony crimes if they had been adults. The juvenile judge scheduled a dispositional hearing to decide what to do with Jeff and Danny. The juvenile judge reviewed the following facts before the dispositional hearing:

Jeff is fifteen years old. He is often truant from school. He has failed one grade level. When he is in school, he often gets into trouble. Jeff lives with his mother and grandmother. His parents are divorced, and he never sees his father anymore. Jeff's mother works during the day. His grandmother has tried to supervise Jeff, but he does not always obey her. Jeff has been in juvenile court on three different occasions: once for curfew violation, once for vandalism, and once for burglary.

Danny is fourteen years old. He lives with his mother and father. He has a good school record and is actually a year ahead of Jeff in school. Danny has only been in juvenile court once before—when he was picked up for curfew violation with Jeff.

YOU BE THE
JUDGE

If you were the judge, what dispositional alternative would you give to Jeff? to Danny? Explain your reasons.

STORY 2

Charlie and Juanita didn't have anything to do one afternoon. They passed a house that no one lived in. "Let's tear the place up," said Juanita. Charlie found an old mattress and with his book of matches, he set it on fire. Someone saw the smoke and called the fire department. As they were running from the house, two police officers caught Charlie and Juanita and took them into custody. Charlie told the police they were just having a good time. They weren't doing anything wrong since no one lived in the house anyway. The police officer said, "It doesn't matter that no one lives in this house. The house is private property, and it is against the law to vandalize it and set it on fire. Arson is a serious crime."

At an adjudicatory hearing, the juvenile judge ruled that Charlie and Juanita had committed the acts as charged—arson and vandalism. Arson is a felony crime for persons treated as adults. The juvenile judge then scheduled a dispositional hearing to decide what to do with Charlie and Juanita. The juvenile judge reviewed the following facts before the hearing:

Charlie is fourteen years old. He lives with his father. His mother died when he was very young. His father works two jobs and does not have much time for Charlie. Charlie is the youngest of three boys in the family. Charlie has about a "C" average in school, and he has not failed any grades. He was taken into juvenile custody once before for setting off fireworks behind the school when he was thirteen.

Juanita is thirteen years old. She lives with her mother and father and five younger sisters and brothers. She often has to take care of the younger children and she sometimes misses school. When she is in school, she makes good grades. She did fail one year because of too many absences—she missed too much work to pass. Juanita has been in juvenile custody on two other occasions—once for running away and once for curfew violation.

YOU BE THE
JUDGE

If you were the judge, what dispositional alternative would you give to Charlie? to Juanita? Explain your reasons.

STORY 3

Mack wanted some spending money. He tried to get a part-time job after school but couldn't find one. A friend, Derrick, said, "A quick way to make a lot of money is to break into houses and steal stereos and TVs. I know people who will take the stolen goods off your hands fast and pay you good money for them." Mack and his friend, Derrick, decided to try it, but eventually they were picked up by the police as they were leaving a home carrying several items.

At the adjudicatory hearing, Mack and Derrick admitted to the juvenile judge that they had committed the burglary of the home and had intended to sell the stolen property (i.e., a TV, VCR, stereo, and gold jewelry). The judge scheduled a dispositional hearing to decide what to do with Mack and Derrick. The judge considered the following facts before the hearing:

Mack is fifteen years old. He is the youngest of two brothers. He lives with his father. His mother abandoned them when he was five. Mack's father drinks a lot and is seldom at home. Mack is a good student and has even made the honor roll. Mack has been in juvenile court twice. Once he was picked up for trespassing on private property. The other time, Mack ran away from home. He told the juvenile officer that he ran away because his father was drunk and beat him up for getting into trouble for trespassing.

Derrick is sixteen years old. He lives with his mother and three younger brothers and sisters. Derrick is seldom home and he often skips school. Derrick recently told his mother he was quitting school. Derrick has been in juvenile custody on several occasions for running away, curfew violations, trespassing, and once for possession with intent to sell marijuana to other students.

YOU BE THE JUDGE

If you were the judge, what dispositional alternatives would you give to Mack? to Derrick? Explain your reasons.

STORY 4

Susan really wanted the latest compact discs (CDs) that some of her friends already had. She had no money. She walked into the Music Shop, took the CDs she wanted, and left. A salesperson ran after her and stopped her as she was going out the door. He called the police. Susan was taken into custody for shoplifting and referred to the juvenile court.

At a later adjudicatory hearing, the juvenile judge determined that Susan had stolen two CDs from the Music Shop. The judge scheduled a dispositional hearing to decide what to do with Susan. The judge has the following information to consider before the hearing:

Susan is thirteen years old. She lives with her mother and father. Susan is an only child, and she is supposed to stay with her grandmother after school and during the summer while her parents work. Susan passes all of her subjects in school, but she was once suspended for stealing some jewelry from another student's locker. Susan had been in juvenile court once before for shoplifting some make-up, but she was only given a warning.

YOU BE THE JUDGE

If you were the judge, what dispositional alternative would you give Susan? Explain your reasons.

In adult criminal courts there are set penalties for crimes. For example, some states have a set penalty of between one and five years in prison for any person convicted of burglary. Penalties are set by federal, state, or local lawmakers. Some people want to change the law so that set penalties would also be given to juveniles who commit offenses. This means that juveniles would be given penalties according to the offense they committed, not according to their individual circumstances.

Should there be set penalties for juveniles based on the seriousness of the offense rather than on the special circumstances of each juvenile?

| EXPLAIN **REASONS FOR** HAVING SET PENALTIES FOR JUVENILES | EXPLAIN **REASONS AGAINST** HAVING SET PENALTIES FOR JUVENILES |

MAKING A DIFFERENCE

You might be interested in learning more about the possible changes your state legislature is considering in the way juvenile courts handle dispositional alternatives. You might write to your state legislator and request information about proposed changes or recent changes in juvenile court procedures in your state. Ask your state legislators to explain to you what they think of these laws (Is he/she planning to vote for them? Why? Why not?). In your letter to your legislator, explain that you are requesting this information because you are preparing a report as part of a school project. Perhaps two or three students could jointly write a letter.

Think about and discuss which questions you most want your state legislators to answer. Don't forget to thank your lawmakers for answering your questions. Your teacher can help you identify the name and address of your state legislators, or you may contact your local library or your county election board to ask for the information. Make copies of your report available for other classes in your school.

· E X T R A ·

Research what the dispositional alternatives are in your area and your state. Your local juvenile court and the library should be able to provide you with this information.

✧ ✧ Vocabulary Words ✧ ✧

mandatory	**restitution**
precedent	**victims**

LESSON 17

The Ultimate Consequence: The Death Penalty

Objectives

As a result of this lesson, students will be able to:

✧ Recognize the importance of the eighth amendment in protecting individuals from cruel and unusual punishments imposed by the government in criminal cases.

✧ Compare and contrast arguments "for" and "against" the death penalty.

✧ Analyze and evaluate the use of the death penalty as a punishment for juveniles.

CASE 1

In your mind, travel back in time 250 years ago. Imagine an adult managing a gang of teen thieves. One of the teens, thirteen-year-old Corey Cooper, snatches a woman's handbag, and dashes off with the handbag clutched in his right hand. Corey is caught, tried, and convicted of robbery. Corey is sentenced to have his right hand cut off and to be placed in the **stocks** in the public square.

Would you consider this to be a fair and reasonable punishment?

Such punishments were not that unusual in the history of our country. Similar punishments, even beheading, are still ordered in some countries around the world.

In your opinion, are these punishments cruel, or are these sentences appropriate for certain convicted criminals? Explain your answer.

Many of the early laws governing the colonies addressed the issue of protecting persons, even animals, from cruel and unusual punishments. For example, the 1641 Massachusetts Body of Liberties stated:

"No man shall be beaten with above 40 stripes, nor shall any true gentleman, nor any man equal to a gentleman be punished with whipping, unless his crime be very shameful..."

"No man shall be forced by torture to confess any crime against himself..."

"For bodily punishments we allow none that are inhumane, barbarous or cruel..."

In debating the need for a Constitutional amendment concerning cruel and unusual punishment, in the *very first* session of the U.S. Congress, one Congressman objected, saying:

> "...it is sometimes necessary to hang a man, villains often deserve whipping, and perhaps having their ears cut off; but are we in the future to be prevented from inflicting these punishments because they are cruel? If a more lenient mode of correcting vice and deterring others from the commission of it would be invented, it would be very prudent in the legislature to adopt it; but until we have some security that this will be done, we ought not to be restrained from making necessary laws by any declaration of this kind."

In the 1791 Bill of Rights of the U.S. Constitution, the eighth amendment states that:

> "Excessive bail shall not be required, nor excessive fines imposed, nor cruel and unusual punishments inflicted."

But what is "**excessive bail**"? And what is "cruel and unusual punishment"?

YOU BE THE JUDGE

Your answers to the questions about what is excessive bail and cruel and unusual punishment may depend on the type of crime committed. For example, you may feel life imprisonment is a cruel punishment for someone found guilty of skipping school, but you may feel that life imprisonment or the **death penalty** is an appropriate punishment for someone found guilty of **premeditated** murder.

Sometimes the United States Supreme Court has been asked to decide if certain punishments are cruel and unusual. Consider the following Texas state law:

The state of Texas passed a law to try to **deter** persons from being repeat offenders. The law states that any person convicted of three or more felonies shall be sentenced to life in prison without parole.

Apply the law to the following case:

Mr. Rummel is caught trying to cash a check for $120.27 in the state of Texas. He knows the check is bad and that he is trying to pay for something without having the money to cover the check. Rummel pleads guilty. This is his third nonviolent felony conviction. The judge applies the new Texas statute against repeat offenders and sentences Rummel to life in prison without parole. Mr. Rummel claims that the sentence violates the Eighth Amendment protection from cruel and unusual punishment. What do you think? Is this a reasonable punishment? Explain your answer.

Mr. Rummel's case went all the way to the United States Supreme Court, *Rummel v. Estelle,* decided in 1980. A majority of the Supreme Court said that a life sentence imposed after a third nonviolent felony is not cruel and unusual. The Court concluded that states have the reserved power and right under the **tenth amendment** of the United States Constitution to establish sentencing guidelines.

CRUEL AND UNUSUAL PUNISHMENT AND THE DEATH PENALTY

Justices of the United States Supreme Court often express differing opinions regarding the death penalty. Every term, the

Supreme Court issues opinions regarding capital punishment. These are literally life and death decisions. Two landmark decisions regarding the death penalty are described below.

Furman v. Georgia

In 1972, in the case of *Furman v. Georgia,* 408 U.S. 238, the Supreme Court's majority ruled that a punishment, like the death penalty, would be "cruel and unusual" and therefore unconstitutional, if the punishment:

✧ Is too severe for the type of crime.

✧ Is inflicted arbitrarily—some get the punishment, others do not, without any guidelines.

✧ Offends society's sense of justice—for example, cutting off someone's head for shouting obscenities.

✧ Is not more effective than a punishment which is less severe.

Using these guidelines, do you think it would be unconstitutional for a state to punish a person for stealing more than $150 in merchandise by sentencing the person to death? Explain your answer.

The majority of the Supreme Court in the *Furman* case decided that the use of the death penalty varied so much from one state to another, that death penalty laws would be unconstitutional unless the laws could overcome the above concerns.

Gregg v. Georgia

Many state legislatures began to write new death penalty laws observing the above guidelines of the *Furman* decision. In 1976, in the case of *Gregg v. Georgia,* 428 U.S. 153, a majority of the U.S. Supreme Court upheld some newly adopted death penalty statutes. They ruled that the death penalty was not always "cruel and unusual punishment." As a matter of fact, at the time the Constitution was ratified, the death penalty was used as a punishment in every state. Even the first United States Congress passed laws providing for the death penalty in certain cases. The Court considered the principal of **federalism** and said state legislatures have the power to determine what punishments are appropriate for the circumstances and crimes in their various states. A state may consider the death penalty as an appropriate punishment for someone found guilty of murder. As long as the death penalty is applied fairly and equally, then each state has the power to use the death penalty as a punishment in **capital crimes.**

Since the Bill of Rights, the United States Supreme Court has given a number of opinions regarding the eighth amendment protection. In 1878, in a case upholding execution by firing squad (*Wilkerson v. Utah*, 99 U.S. 130), the United States Supreme Court said:

> "Punishments of torture (such as drawing and quartering, embowelling alive, beheading, public dissection, and burning alive), and all other in the same line of unconstitutional cruelty, are forbidden by the amendment to the Constitution."

In 1910, in the case of *Weems v. United States*, 217 U.S. 349, Justice Joseph McKenna, writing for the majority of U.S. Supreme Court Justices, said:

> "What constitutes a cruel and unusual punishment has not exactly been decided. It has been said that ordinarily the terms imply something barbarous—torture and the like. But the Eighth Amendment should not be confined to the 'form of evils' that the framers of the Bill of Rights had experienced. . . ."

According to this opinion, the definitions of "cruel and unusual" are subject to changing times.

Keeping in mind the decisions of the U.S. Supreme Court, what would you define as "cruel and unusual" punishment? For example, would it be "cruel or unusual" to sentence someone to jail for the "crime" of being addicted to narcotics? Would it be "cruel or unusual" to sentence a confirmed alcoholic to jail for public drunkenness? Would it be "cruel or unusual" to sentence a person to forty years in prison for possession of nine ounces of marijuana? Explain your answers.

The death penalty itself has not been interpreted by the U.S. Supreme Court to be a "cruel and unusual" punishment. Thirty-eight states have death penalty statutes. Several thousand persons are on death rows awaiting executions. Over the years, some of those waiting to be executed have been juveniles, or they were juveniles at the time of their conviction. We continue to debate whether we should have and use the death penalty. With juveniles facing state execution, there is even more debate about the use of the death penalty.

IDENTIFYING AND ANALYZING ARGUMENTS FOR AND AGAINST THE DEATH PENALTY

Read the statements below. Decide if each statement is an argument FOR or AGAINST the death penalty. Explain at least one argument FOR and one argument AGAINST the death penalty.

1. No other punishment is like the death penalty because of the physical and mental suffering it causes. The death penalty is too brutal.

2. Citizens, as well as a majority of state legislatures, believe the death penalty is an appropriate punishment in some cases. In a democracy the majority rules.

3. Capital punishment expresses society's moral outrage at especially offensive human behavior. It is society's way of saying it will not tolerate cold-blooded murder.

4. The death penalty is an important way to stop crime in some situations.

5. The premeditated taking of a human life by the state is degrading to human dignity. It makes the state no better than the convicted murderer.

6. Killing a human being, when done by any government to carry out a death penalty, is premeditated murder and is uncivilized.

7. If you believe that the cold-blooded killing of a law-abiding citizen is an intolerable crime, you must also believe that the

only just punishment is the giving up of the murderer's own life—a life for a life.

8. The death penalty discriminates against the poor and minorities. It has been applied unfairly against the poor and minorities because when a rich person is found guilty of premeditated murder, he or she is rarely given the death penalty.

9. It is fair for society to get revenge for the death of innocent victims by demanding the execution of the killer, but only after the accused has received due process, a fair trial, and access to all appeal procedures.

10. The United States is the only Western nation that continues to use the death penalty; all other countries (e.g., England, France, West Germany, etc.) have made the death penalty illegal.

Read the summary of the U.S. Supreme Court Case of *Thompson v. Oklahoma*. After studying the following case, YOU BE THE JUDGE and answer the questions that follow on page 164.

THE CASE OF *THOMPSON V. OKLAHOMA*

William Wayne Thompson, along with three adults, **abducted** Charles Keene from a trailer. Keene was Thompson's brother-in-law. They took Keene to the banks of a nearby river and shot, stabbed, and beat him to death. The four of them threw Keene's body into the river. Keene's body was eventually discovered; and Thompson, along with the adults, was arrested and charged with first-degree murder.

Thompson was not yet sixteen years old when he took part in the murder. The state held a transfer hearing to decide if Thompson should be treated as a juvenile or adult. Thompson claimed that he and the others had attacked Keene because Keene had been beating Thompson's sister, to whom Keene was married. The court rejected this claim and certified Thompson to stand trial as an adult.

Thompson was tried by a jury for murder in the first degree—a capital offense in Oklahoma where the murder occurred. In other words, a person found guilty of this crime will be subject to one of two sentences: either the death penalty or life in prison without parole. The jury found Thompson guilty and decided that Keene's murder was especially brutal, monstrous, and cruel; therefore, the jury recommended the death penalty. The judge sentenced Thompson to be executed.

Thompson's Argument

Thompson appealed his conviction and sentence claiming that the sentence violates the eighth amendment. According to Thompson's attorney, the death penalty is cruel as applied to immature juveniles. Thompson's attorney argued that the death penalty is meant to deter someone from committing a cold, **calculated** murder. However, since most teenagers act on impulse, the death penalty for teens serves no reasonable purpose. Furthermore, Thompson's attorney pointed to state laws and U.S. Supreme Court precedents to prove his point that juveniles should be treated differently than adults. Thompson's attorney pointed out that fifteen states have laws that expressly forbid the execution of persons eighteen or younger. Six other states require the sentencing body (in this case the jury) to consider the age of the youth as a **mitigating** factor. Almost all states treat persons under sixteen differently than adults.

In addition, Thompson's attorney cited the 1958 Supreme Court decision in *Trop v. Dulles*: "The meaning of the Eighth Amendment must be drawn from the evolving standards of decency that mark the progress of a maturing society." According to Thompson's attorney, executing juveniles is not a standard of decency in our society. The attorney also said that in 1982, in *Eddings v. Oklahoma,* the Supreme Court considered another juvenile death penalty case and claimed that a judge or jury should consider the defendant's age, family history, and history of emotional disturbance as mitigating factors during the sentencing phase of capital murder cases. Eddings' sentence was changed from the death penalty to life imprisonment without parole. Finally, Thompson's attorney appealed to international law claiming that almost all civilized nations in the Western European community and the Soviet Union prohibit the execution of juveniles.

The State's Argument

The attorney for the state claimed that the power to determine crimes and appropriate sentences (like the death penalty) is a power reserved to the states by the tenth amendment, and this fact is clearly evident since thirty-eight states have capital punishment statutes. Moreover, nineteen states permit the execution of juveniles under sixteen in some circumstances. Most alarming is the fact that ten percent of murders are committed by persons under the age of 18. The death penalty may be a deterrent that will make other juveniles think twice before committing a violent act.

In addition, establishing minimum age standards is another power reserved to the states. States have differing age limits for obtaining a driver's license, getting married, and even attending school. This power should not be taken away from the state.

The attorney for the state also pointed out that the U.S. Supreme Court has declared the death penalty constitutional (see previous section, *Gregg v. Georgia*, page 158). The Court continues to recognize a state's power to use the death penalty as it continues to uphold lower court convictions, and states continue executing persons.

The attorney for the state also claimed that Thompson's age has already been considered as a factor in the transfer (or certification) hearing. If a juvenile is certified to stand trial as an adult, then in the court's opinion, the juvenile is as mature as an adult and should be held accountable for his or her actions, if convicted, just as an adult would be responsible. The use of the death penalty for juveniles may teach other juveniles a lesson to think carefully before they act because the consequences could be fatal. Furthermore, Thompson was only a few days from being sixteen at the time of the murder. If he had been sixteen, he would have automatically been tried for murder as an adult in Oklahoma. A matter of a few days should not allow Thompson to avoid the proper punishment for this terrible homicide.

YOU BE THE JUDGE

1. **FACTS:** What are the important facts in this case? What is the major problem(s)? Who are the sides or parties in this case?

2. **LEGAL ISSUES:** What laws (for example, laws dealing with the U.S. Constitution, state laws or statutes) might apply to this case?

3. **ARGUMENTS:** What arguments would you make for each side in this case?

4. **DECISION:** If you were the judge in this case, what would you decide and why? Would you agree with Thompson and declare the death penalty for juveniles unconstitutional, or would you agree with the state, or would you offer a different opinion? Be sure to explain your decision.

5. **HYPOTHETICAL QUESTIONS:** Would your answer have been different if Thompson had been sixteen at the time of the crime? What if he had been seventeen? eighteen? Explain your answer.

6. **ALTERNATIVE SOLUTIONS:** Are there any other ways of resolving this conflict? For example, should state laws be rewritten regarding capital punishment for juveniles? If your answer is yes, what type of law would you write?

· E X T R A ·

Activity #1

In what year did your state join the United States? Research the criminal laws at the time your state entered the United States. Describe what crimes, if any, would have resulted in capital punishment (the death penalty). Does your state have a death penalty today? If yes, what crimes carry the death penalty as a possible punishment? Compare the use of the death penalty today with capital punishment when your state joined the United States. What changes, if any, have occurred?

Helpful Hint: Contact the research department of your state legislature to help find answers to the above questions.

Activity #2

Contact a member of your state legislature or a representative from the juvenile court, and ask them the following questions:

1. Does (*your state*) have a death penalty statute? If yes, how many persons are on death row in (*your state*)?

2. Can juveniles receive capital punishment in (*your state*)? If yes, are any on death row now?

3. What is your opinion on giving the death penalty to juveniles for certain crimes?

Activity #3

Use the library (or the assistance of an attorney or a legal assistant) to research at least two other U.S. Supreme Court decisions regarding the death penalty. What was the decision of the majority of the Court in each case? Were there any **dissenting opinions**? Briefly explain the dissenting opinions. Write a short story describing situations where someone might receive the death penalty based on the Supreme Court rulings.

Activity #4

Use the library to research the latest U.S. Supreme court decision on juvenile executions, as well as to research and study editorials "for" and "against" the death penalty for juveniles.

✧ ✧ **Vocabulary Words** ✧ ✧

abducted

calculated

capital crimes

death penalty

deter

dissenting opinions

excessive bail

federalism

mitigating

premeditated

stocks

LESSON 18

Consequences of Crime for the Victims and for the Community

Objectives

As a result of this lesson, students will be able to:

✧ Recognize and describe the impact of crime on juvenile and adult victims.

✧ Recognize and describe the impact of crime in the community.

✧ Analyze the short- and long-range consequences of crime on juveniles, adults, and the community.

CONSEQUENCES OF CRIME FOR THE VICTIM

Read the following story and answer the questions that follow.

It was June 15th—a hot, sunny day. School had been out for a little over a week. Fourteen-year-old Sandra and her fifteen-year-old friend, Lisa, were sitting in front of her apartment building. Henry and several of his friends walked by and started to talk to them. A few minutes later, Fred and Allen came by. Fred told Henry that he couldn't talk to Lisa. A fight started. Henry pulled out a gun. During the struggle over the gun, Fred's arm hit Henry's hand, and the shot meant for Fred hit Sandra in the head.

Sandra survived the shot, but she is paralyzed from the neck down and remains in a coma. Her mother, father, brothers, sisters, and other family members and friends come to see her almost daily. They still have hope, but the doctors have warned them that she will never be the same and will need constant care, including nurses and daily therapy (someone moving her muscles to keep them from shrinking). Sandra's love of dancing and dreams of becoming a doctor are gone forever. The hopes and expectations of Sandra's family have changed drastically. The daily routines at home have changed; much of the focus is on Sandra. The family is under a lot of tension and stress because of her condition.   What will happen?

• How was Sandra's life changed on June 15th?

• Who were the victims in this tragedy? How was Sandra's family's life changed? What are the long-range consequences for Sandra's family?

• Has this tragedy affected any other lives? If yes, briefly explain your answer.

• Is there something Sandra could have done to avoid this tragedy? Briefly explain your answer.

Unfortunately, Sandra's story happens too often to too many young teens. When you tune into the news on radio or TV, pick up a newspaper, or hear the sounds of a police siren, crime seems to be everywhere. The United States **Department of Justice** Bureau of Statistics has reported the following frightening fact: Each day, nearly 95,000 crimes are committed—about 66 crimes a minute. That's more than one crime every second.

Teenagers are the most victimized age group when it comes to crimes of **theft** and **violence**. As you are reading this, a teenager is becoming a victim of crime; something is being stolen; a teen is being hit or punched. Crimes happen every second, and they happen to teenagers more often than to any other age group.
The following are stories involving adult crime victims. Read each story and answer the following questions:

Who are the immediate victims in the story? How were the people harmed?

How does this incident affect others? For example, how will the family and friends of those in the story be affected?

What are the costs (including time and money, loss of life, and health, fear, etc.) of this incident to those involved? to the community?

How does this type of story affect you? Briefly explain your answer.

STORY 1

"On my way to the grocery store, two teenage girls knocked me down and stole my purse. I'm 69 years old and live alone. I have no money for my groceries or my medicine. All of my important cards and identification were in my purse. It's going to take a long time to replace everything I lost. Besides being badly bruised when I was knocked down, my glasses were knocked off and broken. I really need my glasses to see; I can't read anything and everything's hazy without them."

STORY 2

"My father was attending a convention. When he was leaving the Convention Center, he was attacked by a gang of teenagers. Someone in the gang hit my father over the head with a ball bat and knocked him unconscious. They took my dad's wallet. He only had three or four dollars. My dad is in a coma, and the doctors told my mom he may have permanent brain damage. He's had two operations, and he may have to have surgery again. I'm the oldest of five children, and I just turned thirteen. I don't know what we will do now."

STORY 3

"I always wanted to be an airline pilot. My parents had helped pay the costs of flight school. I had a good chance at a flying job, and I was going to start paying mom and dad back for putting me through flight school. I had just finished taking the written examination and was driving home. A speeding car, with kids hanging out the window

169

throwing out beer cans, forced me off the highway. My car ran into a tree. The windshield shattered and glass flew into my eyes. The doctors tell me that I'll never see again. My dream of becoming a pilot is lost forever. The medical expenses and adjustments to being blind are unbelievable."

CONSEQUENCES OF CRIME FOR THE COMMUNITY

Crime can also have major consequences for a community. Two crimes, shoplifting and vandalism, which are often committed by juveniles, can harm schools and communities.

One young person gave this example of what can happen as a result of shoplifting:

"My father used to own a grocery store. People from all over the neighborhood shopped there. All the kids came in for candy, apples, potato chips, soda pop—you name it. Shoplifting, especially by a few kids, became a major problem for my dad. He couldn't afford to hire a **security guard** or to install an expensive security system. He didn't want to drive customers away by raising prices, but he had to do something. He finally had enough and shut the store down. My dad said it wasn't just the shoplifting that made

him close down, but that was the straw that broke the camel's back."

Explain what the father meant.

What is the picture below trying to say about shoplifting?

Shoplifting, also called **larceny**, forces stores to raise their prices to pay for their losses. Everyone who buys at the store must pay higher prices for goods in stores where there is frequent shoplifting. Sometimes stores close down or leave a neighborhood because people stop shopping there when prices go up, or because the store loses so much money from having merchandise stolen.

What are some problems people in a neighborhood have when stores move away? What are some of the long-range consequences for the community?

DID YOU KNOW?

In just one year, businesses in the United States lost four billion dollars through shoplifting, internal theft, and bookkeeping errors.

Stores which suffer from shoplifting must pay for burglar alarms, hidden cameras, security guards, and other security systems. The stores raise the prices of their goods in order to have these security systems and still stay in business. Describe who suffers most from shoplifting.

Another frequent crime committed by teens is vandalism. Vandalism is the deliberate, malicious destruction of property. Read the following stories and answer the questions that follow.

"My mother suggested a great family project. We'd all work on fixing up a two-family apartment building. The best apartment building for the money was just ten blocks from our house. We had decided to buy it. We all went back to the building with the real estate agent to have one last look. When we arrived the police were there. They had caught three kids who had vandalized the building. They broke the windows and the water pipes. The water ruined the furnaces. Mom said the cost of fixing the building was too much now. We can't afford the extra expense. I'm so mad. Why did they do such a dumb thing?"

How might this act of vandalism affect this neighborhood? What are the short-range consequences? What are the long-range consequences?

"Our superintendent of schools came into classrooms and explained that the cost of replacing windows and repairing vandalized school property has risen to a new high. The new textbooks planned for the tenth grade cannot be purchased. All field trips will have to be canceled. There just isn't enough money left in the budget. In fact, the superintendent is not even certain that there will be enough money left to pay for the present athletic program. The cost of building materials has risen, and the incidence of vandalism to school buildings just keeps increasing."

How has vandalism affected this school? How would you feel about the vandalism if you were a student at this school? Has your school or school system suffered from vandalism? Describe different types of vandalism that you feel have hurt your school. Describe the short- and long-range consequences of the vandalism for your school.

Does vandalism have any affect on how people feel about your school? Has vandalism affected any of your school programs? Explain your answers.

Activity #1

There are several ways that you and your class can make a difference for crime victims. One way is to find out what agencies or organizations help provide services to crime victims and their families. You could contact one of the **victim assistance** agencies or organizations in your community and find out what kind of help they offer to victims and their families and how you could help.

Another way is to help the agency or organization publicize their services to the community so that more people would benefit from them. You could write a letter to your newspaper explaining how important groups that service crime victims and their families are to the community.

Activity #2

Your class could do a study of the cost of vandalism to your school or school system. Talk to your principal about the idea. With his/her permission write to the superintendent of your school system. Ask for information on vandalism to the schools during the last few years. The building department might have detailed figures showing the cost of repairing broken windows and other destroyed property. How would broken windows affect heating costs? What about the cost of removing the writing on walls in the buildings? How many desks have to be replaced because of deliberate damage?

You could compare the cost of textbooks or athletic supplies to the cost of vandalism at your school. What could the system buy for students if it did not have to spend so much on vandalism?

When your class completes its report, send a copy to the principal and ask what he or she would like to do with the report. For example, you might hold a meeting to present the results of your study to the entire school or to the parent association. The next step would be to develop and implement a plan with the principal, your teacher, and others to reduce vandalism in your school.

· EXTRA ·

Activity #1

Read the newspaper for several days and find stories concerning crimes. Select one of the articles and write a story about how you think the crime victim(s) and his or her family felt. Also describe in your story how the crime might have changed the lives of the victim(s) for years to come.

Activity #2

Research the most current crime statistics through your local law enforcement agency or the United States Department of Justice. What crimes are occurring most frequently in your community? Brainstorm ideas for reducing crime in your community.

✦ ✦ Vocabulary Words ✦ ✦

Department of Justice   **theft**
larceny   **victim assistance**
security guard   **violence**

LESSON 19

Juveniles Against Crime

Objectives

As a result of this lesson, students will be able to:

✧ Identify and discuss some of the causes of juvenile crime.

✧ Identify and discuss ways that they as individuals and as a class can fight juvenile crime.

People concerned with juvenile delinquency have many different views on what causes juvenile crime and how to stop juveniles from committing crimes.

Can you think of what some of these might be?

One of these views says that in order to prevent juvenile crime, juveniles themselves must be actively involved in the crime prevention process.

Do you agree with this view? Why or why not?

In order to get involved in the prevention process, you must first look at the causes of juvenile crime. As a class, develop a list of some of the reasons why young people break the law.

WHY YOUNG PEOPLE BREAK THE LAW

Now go over your list of reasons and for each one you named, suggest some action that might help prevent the juvenile crime, or that might help a juvenile overcome a problem without breaking the law. For example, if one of the reasons for getting into illegal activity is:

"All of my friends do it". . . *then*

Can you suggest some ways of overcoming this problem without breaking the law?

Brainstorm positive suggestions and solutions for each of the reasons you identified.

Below is a list of illegal acts often committed by juveniles. Several reasons are given for each illegal act. Imagine you are going to survey young people to identify their opinions regarding these reasons. On a separate sheet of paper, rank the reasons that young people might give for committing each offense, beginning with what you believe would be the most frequently given reasons. If you think of a reason not already listed, include that reason in a space marked "other". In column two on your paper suggest a way of preventing this type of illegal act.

Column 1	**Column 2**
Offenses and possible reasons	
1. Juveniles *shoplift* because:	Based on your first-ranked answer, what can be done to prevent *shoplifting?*
they need what they take.	
it's a challenge not to get caught.	
they feel the store can afford the loss.	
they know they won't get a stiff penalty if they are caught.	
other	

2. Juveniles use *illegal drugs:*

   to escape from their personal problems.

   to be accepted.

   to do what their friends do.

   because they see their parents using alcohol and other drugs.

   other

Based on your first-ranked answer, what can be done to prevent the illegal use of *drugs?*

3. Juveniles *destroy property (vandalize):*

   because they are angry and don't know how else to show it.

   to get back at someone.

   for fun.

   because they have owned very few things and probably don't know how it feels to have something you own destroyed.

   other

Based on your first-ranked answer, what can be done to prevent *vandalism?*

4. Juveniles commit **assault and battery:**

   to prove they are tough.

   because they don't know how to talk out problems or anger.

   because picking on people makes them feel big.

   because they were beaten when they were younger.

   other

Based on your first-ranked answer, what can be done to prevent *assault* or *assault and battery?*

As a class, discuss the number one reason given for each of the four illegal acts. Did most people rank the same reason first? Were the suggested ways of preventing illegal acts realistic? Explain your answers.

IMAGINE THAT BECAUSE OF YOUR EXCELLENT WORK ON THE PREVIOUS PAGES, the governor of your state has just contacted you and has asked you to serve on the Governor's Commission on Juvenile Crime Prevention. You are to turn in a report, working in a group of other selected commission members. Your report should include suggestions on how to deter young people from committing different kinds of offenses. Describe in detail how your suggestions would work. Also, answer the following questions and explain your answers in your report and develop additional questions and responses.

✦ Should there be set penalties for juveniles? Would that reduce crime? Why or why not?

✦ Should more money be spent for rehabilitation programs? Why or why not? What kinds of programs do you think would be most effective? Why?

✦ Should anyone over 14 found delinquent of a felony be tried as an adult? Why or why not?

✦ Should more money be put into prevention programs for young people? What kinds of programs? Why?

✦ Should there be a program for restitution in juvenile courts? Why or why not? How would it work? What kinds of offenses would be included? Why?

Develop a plan of action to help prevent and fight juvenile crime. In developing your plan, research what is currently being done in your city and state to prevent and fight juvenile crime. Does your city have a crime prevention council or commission? Your state? Your mayor, governor, attorney general, and community agencies may have programs, councils, and commissions to prevent and fight crime. Collecting information on what is already being done will help you to decide what your own role can be in juvenile crime prevention.

You could share your plan of action in several different ways.

1. Send a copy of your report to your local or state crime prevention agency. Encourage the agency to respond or comment on your report.

2. After sending your report, contact your local or state crime prevention agency and ask for a speaker to come out to your school and discuss the agency's response to your report. The speaker could talk to your class and other classes or to a meeting of your school's parent organization.

3. Use your report as a basis for a Juvenile Crime Prevention Conference. You could invite the governor or **attorney general** or representatives from their offices, local and state law enforcement officers, and others to discuss your report and help you work on preventing and fighting juvenile crime.

· **E X T R A** ·

Contact the local or state crime prevention agency and request information on what the agency is doing to prevent and fight crime.

✧ ✧ **Vocabulary Words** ✧ ✧

assault and battery   **attorney general**

BILL OF RIGHTS

Amendment 1 (1791)

Freedom of religion, speech, and press; peaceful assemblage; petition of grievances

Congress shall make no law respecting an establishment of religion, or prohibiting the free exercise thereof; or abridging the freedom of speech, or of the press, or the right of the people peaceably to assemble, and to petition the Government for a redress of grievances.

Amendment 2 (1791)

State militias and bearing arms

A well regulated Militia, being necessary to the security of a free State, the right of the people to keep and bear Arms, shall not be infringed.

Amendment 3 (1791)

Quartering of soldiers in homes

No Soldier shall, in time of peace be quartered in any house, without the consent of the Owner, nor in time of war, but in a manner to be prescribed by law.

Amendment 4 (1791)

Searches and seizures

The right of the people to be secure in their persons, houses, papers, and effects, against unreasonable searches and seizures, shall not be violated, and no Warrants shall issue, but upon probable cause, supported by Oath or affirmation, and particularly describing the place to be searched, and the persons or things to be seized.

Amendment 5 (1791)

Capital crimes; double jeopardy; self-incrimination; due process; eminent domain; just compensation for property

No person shall be held to answer for a capital, or otherwise infamous crime, unless on a presentment or indictment of a Grand Jury, except in cases arising in the land or naval forces, or in the Militia, when in actual service in time of War or public danger; nor shall any person be subject for the same offence to be twice put in jeopardy of life or limb nor shall be compelled in any criminal case to be a witness against himself, nor be deprived of life, liberty, or property, without due process of law; nor shall private property be taken for public use without just compensation.

Amendment 6 (1791)

Jury trial for crimes, and procedural rights of the accused

In all criminal prosecutions, the accused shall enjoy the right to a speedy and public trial, by an impartial jury of the State and district wherein the crime shall have been committed; which district shall have been previously ascertained by law, and to be informed of the nature and cause of the accusation; to be confronted with the witnesses against him; to have compulsory process for obtaining witnesses in his favor, and to have the assistance of counsel for his defence.

Amendment 7 (1791)

Civil trials

In Suits at common law, where the value in controversy shall exceed twenty dollars, the right of trial by jury shall be preserved, and no fact tried by a jury shall be otherwise re-examined in any Court of the United States, than according to the rules of the common law.

Amendment 8 (1791)

Excessive bail, fines, punishments for crimes

Excessive bail shall not be required, nor excessive fines imposed, nor cruel and unusual punishments inflicted.

Amendment 9 (1791)

Other rights retained by the people

The enumeration in the Constitution of certain rights shall not be construed to deny or disparage others retained by the people.

Amendment 10 (1791)

Reserved powers to states

The powers not delegated to the United States by the Constitution, nor prohibited by it to the States, are reserved to the States respectively, or to the people.

GLOSSARY

abandoning a child	Deserting a child; leaving a child without support.
abduct	Taking someone by force or holding them against their will; to kidnap.
abused	Treated badly, either physically or mentally. This term is often used in reference to abused and neglected children who are suffering serious physical or emotional injury, including malnutrition.
accomplice	A person who knowingly and voluntarily assists the principal offender in committing a crime. A person may be charged as an accomplice if he or she is present and aiding or abetting another in committing the crime, or by advising or encouraging someone to commit the crime.
action(s)	Something that is or has been done.
adjudicatory	To settle a conflict using the judicial branch of government.
adjudicatory hearing	A hearing to decide whether or not a juvenile committed the offense of which he or she is accused. The facts of the case are brought out by evidence presented at the hearing, including questioning of the juvenile and other witnesses.

aggravated assault | A person is guilty of aggravated assault if he or she attempts to cause serious bodily injury to another, or knowingly acts in a reckless manner which creates a serious risk of death and causes serious physical injury to another.

allegation | A declaration or statement of a person explaining or describing what he or she expects to prove.

alternative | A choice between two or more things or courses of action.

amendment(s) | An addition to or change in a bill, statute, or constitution.

analyze | To study and carefully consider all sides of a situation or problem in an effort to reach a solution.

appeal | Take a case to a higher court for a rehearing.

appropriate | Useful and fitting to the proper circumstances or needs.

armed robbery | A form of robbery in which the defendant is armed with a deadly weapon.

arrested | Seized and held by authority of law. A person is arrested when he or she is suspected of a crime and taken into custody.

arson | The deliberate and purposeful burning of property.

assault | A threat and/or act carried out to use force on and harm another person.

attorney general	The head of the U.S. Department of Justice and chief law officer of the federal government. He or she (or subordinates) represents the United States in legal matters and gives advice and opinions to the president and to the heads of other executive departments of the federal government when requested. In each state there is also an attorney general, who is the chief legal officer of the state.
bail	Money, or some form of security (like a deed of property) that the judge makes the accused person leave with the court in order to be released before the next appearance in court. If the accused fails to appear in court he or she forfeits the bail.
bailiff	An officer of the court responsible for keeping order, who has charge of the accused person while he or she is in the courtroom, and who also looks after the jurors.
battery	Any intentional, harmful physical contact by one person upon another, without that person's consent.
beyond a reasonable doubt	The level of proof required to convict a person of a crime. It does not mean "convinced one hundred percent," but does mean there are no reasonable doubts as to guilt.
bill	A draft of a law presented to a legislature for consideration.
Bill of Rights	A formal declaration of rights and liberties often found in state constitutions, and the first ten amendments to the United States Constitution. These amendments express certain rights of the people which are considered fundamental, such as freedom of speech.

brainstorm(ed)	To develop ideas without necessarily worrying about how good or practical they may be; a free flow of ideas without comment or criticism.
branches of government	The three different divisions of the government—legislative, executive, and judicial. The legislative branch makes the laws, the executive branch carries out the laws, and the judicial branch interprets the laws.
breaking and entering	A term used to describe a criminal act which consists of forcible entry to the building of another, residential or commercial, with the intent to commit a crime.
calculate(d)	Plan(ned) in advance.
capital crime(s)	Offense(s) which may be punishable by death or life imprisonment.
capital punishment	The death penalty.
certification	The judicial process by which a juvenile is certified to stand trial as an adult. Also called a transfer hearing.
certified	A certified juvenile is one who is treated as an adult. The certified juvenile is transferred from juvenile jurisdiction to adult criminal jurisdiction.
child abuse	Child abuse is defined generally in terms of actions taken by a child's parent or guardian which actively and intentionally hurt the child. The actions may include physical, emotional or mental cruelty. A parent's beating of a five-year-old child with an iron

rod or locking a child in a dark closet for 24 hours at a time are examples.

child welfare
A general term referring to the measures necessary to support a child's overall well-being: physical, emotional and mental needs.

cite
To read or refer to cases, law, or other legal information. For example, an attorney might cite a particular court case in support of his or her client.

clear and convincing evidence
Generally, this phrase and its numerous variations mean proof beyond a reasonable or well-founded doubt.

clerk
Court official who keeps court records and official files.

competent witness
A person who is legally qualified to give testimony in a case. Someone who is capable of understanding and responding to questions in a court-related proceeding.

confidence
Information that is not revealed to others and is kept secret.

confrontation
The constitutional right of a defendant, in most cases, to come face to face with a witness, and to be able to cross-examine the witness.

Congress
The branch of the government of the United States that makes laws. Congress is made up of the Senate and the House of Representatives.

consequence
The result or outcome of some action or set of conditions.

court reporter	A legal stenographer who records court proceedings.
crime(s)	An act that is forbidden by law, or failure to do an act that the law requires.
criminal code	The laws of the state or federal government defining crimes and punishment.
curfew	A law, usually a local ordinance, which requires persons under a certain age (juveniles) to be off the streets before a certain time of night.
custody	The care and keeping of something or someone, such as a child.
death penalty	The punishment in some states and by the federal government of executing a person convicted of a crime that resulted in the death of another person. In most cases, the death penalty is only imposed if the defendant is found guilty of premeditated murder.
decision(s)	The act or result of making up one's mind.
defense attorney	The lawyer who represents a defendant (that is, someone who has a complaint filed against him or her in a court of law), in civil or criminal cases.
delinquent	A child who has committed an act that, if committed by an adult, would be a crime under federal, state, or local law. The term is also used to describe juveniles found by the juvenile court to be incorrigible, or in need of supervision.
democracy	A form of government in which supreme power is held by the people and is exercised by them or their representatives who are elected by the free choice of the people.

Department of Justice	One of the executive departments of the federal government, headed by the attorney general. This department is responsible for enforcing federal laws and providing legal counsel in all federal cases. It gives legal advice and opinions to the president and to the heads of other executive departments. It also supervises the federal prison system.
detention center	A place where juveniles are held (in detention) while awaiting a hearing.
deter	To discourage or stop, usually by fear.
deterrent	A reason for punishment based on the belief that the punishment will discourage the offender from committing another crime in the future and will serve as an example to keep other people from committing crimes.
discretion	A power or right granted to a person to exercise his or her own judgment in certain circumstances. Discretion should be guided by the spirit and principles of the law.
discriminate	To distinguish between; to treat differently.
disposition	The final settlement or result of a case. A term used in juvenile court; similar to a sentence in adult court.
dispositional hearing	A proceeding to decide what should be done with a juvenile who has been found to be delinquent.
dissenting opinion	A decision that disagrees with other decisions on a similar topic or issue; often refers to a judge's or judges' disagreement with the decisions of a majority of other judges.

driving while intoxicated (DWI)	A serious crime committed by one who operates a motor vehicle while under the influence of intoxicating liquor or drugs.
due process	Procedures to protect individual rights in legal proceedings.
due process hearing	An orderly proceeding where a person is notified of the details of a case, and where the person has an opportunity to be heard and to enforce and protect his or her rights before the authority having power to hear and decide the case. The proceeding follows the standards of fairness and justice.
DWI	See "driving while intoxicated". An abbreviation for "driving while intoxicated."
embezzlement	The taking of money or property by a person who has been entrusted with it, such as a bank teller or a company accountant.
empathy	Ability to share in another's emotions or feelings.
endangering the welfare of a child	Putting the well-being of a child in danger or in harm's way.
enforce(d)	To make certain that a law or rule is carried out; to force others to obey.
evaluating	Determining whether actions taken have helped to achieve a goal or solved a problem.
evidence	Any material of proof presented in a legal case to help find the truth. Evidence may include witnesses, records, documents, exhibits, and other physical objects that provide the facts of a case.

excessive	Conduct or behavior that goes beyond that which is normal, proper, or necessary.
excessive bail	The eighth amendment to the U.S. Constitution prohibits excessive bail, an amount that is more than would be reasonable to assure that the accused returns for the next court appearance.
executive	The branch of government responsible for enforcing or carrying out the laws.
expectation(s)	Something which will probably happen or which is anticipated to happen.
federal	Relating to the government of the United States of America, organized under the Constitution of the United States.
federalism	The relationship between the states and the federal government; the federal system that establishes the power of the federal government and state governments.
felon	Someone who commits a felony (a very serious crime such as murder or armed robbery with a sentence of a year or more in prison).
felony	A very serious crime such as murder or armed robbery punishable by a sentence of a year or more in prison.
fine	A sum of money to be paid as a punishment by a person convicted of an offense. The money penalty may be in addition to a jail or prison sentence.
foster care	Care provided to a child who is without parents or who has been removed from the custody of his or her parents.

fourteenth amendment	This amendment to the United States Constitution was ratified in 1868. It defines citizenship, and is often emphasized for protecting persons or groups of people from unfair government action, and providing persons with "due process" and "equal protection of the laws."
fraud	Any intentional deception, lie, or dishonest statement made to cheat someone.
goal(s)	An aim that one strives to achieve.
guardian ad litem	A person (usually a lawyer) who is appointed by a court to take care of the interests of someone during a lawsuit or hearing.
guilty	The word used by an accused in pleading or confessing wrong-doing; the word used by a judge or a jury in convicting a defendant charged with a particular crime.
hearing	A relatively formal proceeding, sometimes in a trial-like setting, to examine matters of fact or law.
House of Representatives	Usually refers to the lower chamber of the Congress of the United States. There are 435 representatives from the fifty states in the U.S. House of Representatives. The number of representatives from each state is determined by population, and every state is entitled to at least one representative.
identifying	Selecting an alternative from one or more choices.
incorrigible	Incapable of being corrected, reformed, or improved. With respect to juvenile offenders, this refers to parents or legal guardians claiming that their son or daughter is no

longer manageable, and unable to be properly controlled.

indeterminate	Not exactly determined; not known in advance.
influence	To try to persuade someone to do something.
interpret	Usually refers to the process of discovering or determining the meaning of a point of law (for example, a statute, will, contract, or other legal document — even constitutions). Judges are sometimes called upon to make legal interpretations.
judge	A public official appointed or elected whose duty it is to decide questions of law brought before a court and to make certain that legal procedures are followed.
judicial	Relating to courts of law or judges.
jurisdiction	In judicial jurisdiction, a term which means the places and types of cases over which a court has authority to hear and decide.
juvenile(s)	A young person, not yet an adult. State laws establish the age for juveniles and the age at which the juvenile becomes an adult.
juvenile code	A special set of laws applying to young people.
juvenile court	A court set up to handle the cases concerning young people.
kidnapping	The forcible abduction or carrying away of a person by another person. This is a serious felony.

larceny	Intentionally stealing or taking another's personal property. It is usually a felony.
law(s)	A rule made by a government.
lawmaker(s)	Members of the legislative branch of government who introduce and assist in passing laws for local, state, and federal governments. Commonly referred to as "legislators."
legislative	Having the power or authority to make laws.
levels of government	Local, state, or federal governing bodies.
lobbying	Influencing or persuading legislators to take action to introduce a bill or vote a certain way on a proposed law.
lobbyist	A person who tries to influence the members of a legislative body to vote for or against a particular bill.
local	Referring to laws or ordinances of the governing body of a community or county.
long-range consequence(s)	An end result of some action that occurs much later than the action itself.
mandatory	A command or obligation; something that must be done.
manslaughter	The unlawful killing of another without malice. Manslaughter may be either voluntary or involuntary.
minor(s)	A person too young to take on the legal rights and duties of an adult. In most jurisdictions, a person under a certain age, usually 18, is considered a minor by law.

misdemeanor	A less serious crime where the imprisonment cannot be for more than one year.
mitigating	Circumstances that may be considered in determining someone's responsibility for committing a wrong.
murder	The unlawful and intentional killing of a person. A person commits murder if he or she intentionally, knowingly, and deliberately causes the death of another person.
neglect	Neglect is generally defined as action by a parent or guardian which places the child in a dangerous situation.
neglected	Treated with neglect (see above definition).
offender(s)	A person involved in committing a crime or breaking the law.
offense(s)	A term used for a violation of the law in juvenile and adult criminal jurisdictions.
ordinance	A law, usually made by a city or county level of government.
parens patriae	The principle of law under which the court protects the interests of a juvenile.
peer(s)	A person of approximately the same age, rank, or standing as another. The phrase "trial by a jury of his or her peers" has been interpreted to mean "tried by a jury of citizens."
penal	Relating to a penalty or punishment, like being sentenced to a penal institution or prison.

perspective(s)	Your own or another's way of looking at a situation or problem.
petition	A formal request, usually in writing, to a person or persons in authority.
petty theft	Also known as "petty larceny." A term used to describe the crime of stealing or taking of property or services of another without permission or by means of deceit when the value of the stolen property is less than a certain amount, usually $150.
practice	The usual way of doing things.
precedents	Previous court decisions used for guidance in deciding questions of law in similar cases.
preliminary hearing	Pretrial proceeding at which the prosecutor must prove to a judge that a crime was committed and establish the probable guilt of the defendant.
premeditated	Planned ahead of time. To think about something before doing it. The term is often used to describe an element in a first degree murder charge—"the defendant thought about and planned to commit the murder before doing it."
pressure	Physical, psychological, or social force intended to result in a certain kind of behavior.
probable cause	A reasonable belief, known personally or through reliable sources, that a person has committed a crime. Probable cause is a requirement needed for search warrants as expressed in the Fourth Amendment to the U.S. Constitution.

probation	A sentence releasing a defendant into the community under the supervision of a probation officer. This sentence usually requires the defendant to obey certain conditions—for example, be on good behavior, do not break the law, and report to the probation officer as required.
process	A series of steps or actions that lead to or bring about a result.
prohibit	To forbid or prevent.
prosecute(d)	To bring a person to trial on criminal charges and to pursue the case to its conclusion.
prosecuting attorney	Lawyer or attorney who defends the interest and rights of the people of a state or federal government against the defendant in a criminal trial.
punishment	A penalty for a crime or wrongdoing.
rape	Unlawful sexual relations with a female, or in most jurisdictions male or female, without her or his consent.
reasonable suspicion	Having some reliable evidence to believe that an act has been committed. It is more than a guess but less than probable cause.
refusal skills	Skills that help one to say "no" to becoming involved in actions that are not responsible.
rehabilitation	The restoration of a person to a way of life which is acceptable to society.
repeal(ing)	To officially do away with an authority and/or law that had previously been followed.

requirement(s)	Something that is necessary or demanded.
resource(s)	People, places or materials that one can turn to for support or help.
responsible	Able to answer for one's own behavior; receiving the credit or blame for one's acts or decisions; dependable and trustworthy. Under the law, this term is used to describe liability. A party (person or group) is held legally accountable or answerable for his or her behavior.
responsibility	The state of being responsible.
restitution	A type of sentence or disposition in which the lawbreaker is ordered to repay the victim for his or her loss or for harm done to him or her.
right to confrontation	A term used to describe the right of a person to face a witness who may be testifying against this person. The right to face a witness also means that a person has a right to ask questions of the witness (see "right to cross-examination"). This right is guaranteed by the state constitutions and United States Constitution sixth amendment.
right to cross-examination	During a trial, a hearing, or in taking a deposition (witness statement), a person, or his or her attorney, has the right to ask questions of an opposing witness. For example, if a witness testifies against a defendant during a trial or hearing, the defendant, or his or her attorney, has the right to confront and ask the witness questions.
robbery	The unlawful taking of property from a person's immediate possession by force or threat of force.
rule(s)	A guide or principle for conduct or action.

safeguard	A specific way to protect a right or freedom.
security guard	A person employed to supervise or provide security or protection for a certain area.
self-esteem	Respect that one holds for oneself.
self-incrimination	A term used to describe a person's confession to criminal behavior. The fifth amendment to the U.S. Constitution as well as most state constitutions prohibits the government from compelling or making a person testify or give evidence against himself or herself.
sentence(s)	The punishment or penalty given by the judge to a person who has pleaded guilty to a crime or who has been found guilty by a jury or judge.
shoplifting	The crime of stealing merchandise from a store or business establishment.
short-range consequence(s)	An end result of some action that occurs soon after the action itself.
simple assault	The crime of striking or attempting to strike another person with the intent of inflicting injury to that person without reasonable justification.
solve	Find an answer or solution.
state	One of the political and geographic subdivisions of the United States. A state is different from local and federal levels of government.
status offender	One who is in violation of a law which applies only to juveniles.

statute	A law, usually made by a legislature.
stocks	A form of public punishment. Specifically it refers to a wooden framework with holes for ankles or for the ankles and wrists, and sometimes the head, that was once used to punish wrongdoers in a public place.
strategy	A planned way of achieving a goal.
taken into custody	A term used in juvenile law similar to arrest in an adult criminal proceeding.
testify	To make an official statement or give evidence under oath, to help establish the truth or prove some fact.
testimony	The information a witness gives under oath.
theft	The crime of taking property or services without the owner's consent. Another term for theft is "larceny."
theory	One or more ideas which explain how something is supposed to happen.
trial	A proceeding in a court for the purpose of settling a legal problem by considering evidence on both sides.
truant	A minor who is absent from school without permission.
unconstitutional	Not legal because it is in conflict with a state constitution or the United States Constitution, and is delared unconstitutional by a higher court.
United States Constitution	The fundamental and highest law of the United States, setting forth the basic principles and framework of our federal govern-

ment. All fifty states have state constitutions that set forth the principles and framework of each state's government.

United States Senate
The name of the upper chamber of the Congress of the United States. Each state is represented by two senators in the U.S. Senate.

United States Supreme Court
The highest federal court in the United States.

vandalism
The deliberate destruction of property.

vehicular homicide
Similar to the crime of vehicular manslaughter; referring to any death caused by the illegal operation of a motor vehicle. For example, the illegal operation may refer to intentional conduct or negligence on the part of the driver that caused a person's death.

vehicular injury
A crime referring to an injury to another person caused by the operation of a motor vehicle by someone driving under the influence of drugs/alcohol and/or driving recklessly. For example, a person may be charged with committing "vehicular injury" if the person, driving while intoxicated, hits and injures another person.

vehicular manslaughter
A serious felony. Committing or causing the death of another person by the operation of a motor vehicle by someone driving under the influence of drugs/alcohol and driving recklessly. For example, a person may be charged with committing "vehicular manslaughter or homicide" if the person, driving while intoxicated, hits and causes the death of another person.

victim
The person against whom a criminal act is committed.

victim assistance	Usually refers to aid that is offered from public and/or private agencies to victims of crime. Almost all states have passed laws to aid victims of crime.
violate	Break the law.
violence	Under the law, this refers to any unjust or unwarranted use of force. Committing a violent act, like an assault, is a felony.
writ of habeas corpus	A procedure by which a person already in prison petitions to have the case reconsidered by a higher court. The writ directs the prison authorities who "Have the Body" of the prisoner to produce it for the hearing.